Discover Malaysia

AVERY B. HODGES

Published by AVERY B. HODGES, 2023.

While every precaution has been taken in the preparation of this book, the publisher assumes no responsibility for errors or omissions, or for damages resulting from the use of the information contained herein.

DISCOVER MALAYSIA

First edition. October 7, 2023.

Copyright © 2023 AVERY B. HODGES.

ISBN: 979-8223945147

Written by AVERY B. HODGES.

Table of Contents

Chapter 1: Introduction to Malaysia

Welcome to Malaysia, a country that boasts a rich tapestry of diverse cultures, breathtaking landscapes, and a fascinating history. Situated in Southeast Asia, Malaysia is known for its vibrant cities, pristine beaches, lush rainforests, and warm hospitality. In this chapter, we will provide you with a brief overview of the country, including its geography, history, culture, and attractions, allowing you to embark on a memorable journey through this enchanting land.

Geography:

Malaysia is located on the Malay Peninsula and the island of Borneo, with the South China Sea separating it from the Philippines and Vietnam. The country's diverse topography ranges from towering mountains such as Mount Kinabalu to dense rainforests, stunning coastlines, and idyllic islands. With a tropical climate, Malaysia is blessed with abundant flora and fauna, making it a paradise for nature lovers.

History:

The history of Malaysia is a tapestry woven with influences from various civilizations. From the ancient Malay kingdoms to the Portuguese, Dutch, and British colonial periods, Malaysia's past is a testament to its resilience and multicultural heritage. The country gained independence in 1957 and has since developed into a thriving nation, embracing its cultural diversity while preserving its historical landmarks.

Culture:

Malaysia's cultural mosaic is a blend of Malay, Chinese, Indian, and indigenous traditions. This unique fusion is reflected in its architecture, cuisine, festivals, and customs. Malaysians are known for their warm hospitality, and visitors will be delighted by the harmonious coexistence of different ethnicities, religions, and languages. From the vibrant street markets of Kuala Lumpur to the serene villages of Sarawak, Malaysia offers a captivating cultural experience.

Attractions:

Malaysia is a treasure trove of attractions that cater to every traveler's taste. The bustling capital city, Kuala Lumpur, is home to iconic landmarks like the Petronas Twin Towers and the vibrant street of Jalan Alor, renowned for its delectable street food. The UNESCO World Heritage Site of George Town in Penang showcases a fusion of colonial and Asian architectural styles, while the pristine beaches of Langkawi and the Perhentian Islands offer a tranquil escape. For wildlife enthusiasts, the jungles of Borneo are home to rare species such as orangutans and proboscis monkeys.

As you embark on your journey through Malaysia, prepare to be captivated by its natural wonders, immersed in its rich history, and enchanted by its cultural diversity. This introduction merely scratches the surface of what this extraordinary country has to offer. So, pack your bags, open your mind, and get ready to create memories that will last a lifetime in the enchanting land of Malaysia.

Note: This chapter provides a brief overview of Malaysia and its attractions. For more detailed information, please refer to the subsequent chapters dedicated to specific regions, cities, and attractions within the country.

Chapter 2: When to Visit Malaysia

Malaysia, a vibrant and culturally diverse country, offers a plethora of experiences for tourists throughout the year. From stunning landscapes and pristine beaches to bustling cities and rich heritage, Malaysia has something for everyone. However, to make the most of your trip, it is essential to plan your visit according to the best time for your desired activities and preferences. In this chapter, we will provide you with valuable tips for planning when to go on a tourist trip to Malaysia.

1. Weather Considerations:

Malaysia experiences a tropical climate, characterized by high humidity and temperatures ranging between 25°C to 35°C (77°F to 95°F) throughout the year. However, the country also has two distinct monsoon seasons that can affect your travel plans. The Southwest Monsoon, known as the wet season, occurs from May to September, bringing heavy rainfall to the western coast, including popular destinations like Penang and Langkawi. On the other hand, the Northeast Monsoon, from November to March, affects the eastern coast, including the beautiful islands of Perhentian and Tioman. To avoid excessive rainfall, plan your visit during the dry season, which is generally from April to October.

2. Festivals and Cultural Events:

Malaysia is renowned for its vibrant festivals and cultural celebrations, which offer a unique insight into the country's diverse heritage. If you wish to immerse yourself in the local culture, plan your visit around these events. The most significant festival in Malaysia is Hari Raya Aidilfitri, also known as Eid al-Fitr, which marks the end of Ramadan. This celebration usually takes place in June or July and offers a wonderful opportunity to witness traditional customs and enjoy delectable Malay cuisine. Other notable festivals include Chinese New Year, Thaipusam, and the Rainforest World Music Festival. Check the calendar of events before planning your trip to experience the cultural richness of Malaysia.

3. Wildlife Encounters:

For nature enthusiasts, Malaysia is a paradise teeming with diverse flora and fauna. If you are keen on wildlife encounters, it is crucial to plan your visit accordingly. The best time to spot orangutans and other wildlife in Borneo's rainforests is during the dry season, from March to October. In contrast, the wet season, from November to February, can make trekking and jungle exploration challenging due to heavy rainfall. Similarly, if you dream of witnessing the majestic sea turtles nesting on the beaches of Terengganu, plan your visit between May and September.

4. Budget Considerations:

The cost of accommodation and flights can vary depending on the time of year you visit Malaysia. The peak tourist season in Malaysia generally coincides with school holidays, major festivals, and favorable weather conditions. This period, from December to February and June to August, witnesses higher prices for flights and accommodations. To make your trip more budget-friendly, consider visiting during the shoulder seasons, such as April to May or September to November. During these periods, you can still enjoy pleasant weather while benefiting from lower prices and fewer crowds.

Remember, the best time to visit Malaysia ultimately depends on your interests, preferred activities, and budget. By considering the weather, festivals, wildlife encounters, and budget considerations, you can plan a memorable trip to Malaysia that aligns perfectly with your expectations.

Chapter 3: What to Pack for Your Trip to Malaysia

Malaysia, a vibrant and diverse country located in Southeast Asia, offers a plethora of experiences for every type of traveler. From its bustling cities to its stunning beaches and lush rainforests, Malaysia has something for everyone. As you prepare for your trip to this enchanting destination, it is crucial to pack wisely to ensure a comfortable and enjoyable journey. Here are some essential items to include in your packing list:

1. Lightweight and Breathable Clothing:

Malaysia's tropical climate means that the weather is generally hot and humid throughout the year. Pack lightweight and breathable clothing, such as cotton or linen, to stay cool and comfortable. Don't forget to include a hat, sunglasses, and sunscreen to protect yourself from the intense sun rays.

2. Rain Gear:

Although Malaysia enjoys a tropical climate, it is also known for occasional rain showers. Be prepared by packing a foldable umbrella or a lightweight waterproof jacket. This way, you can continue exploring even during a sudden downpour.

3. Comfortable Footwear:

With numerous attractions and activities to explore, comfortable footwear is a must. Opt for breathable and sturdy shoes or sandals that are suitable for walking long distances. If you plan to hike in the rainforests, consider packing a pair of hiking boots or shoes with good traction.

4. Insect Repellent:

Malaysia is home to a variety of insects, including mosquitoes. Protect yourself from potential bites by packing an effective insect repellent. Look for a product that contains DEET or other recommended ingredients to ensure maximum protection.

5. Travel Adapters:

Malaysia uses Type G electrical outlets, so it is essential to pack a universal travel adapter to charge your electronics. This will allow you to stay connected and keep your devices powered up throughout your trip.

6. Medications and First Aid Kit:

If you take any prescription medications, be sure to pack an adequate supply for the duration of your trip. Additionally, it is advisable to bring a basic first aid kit containing essentials such as band-aids, antiseptic cream, and any personal medications you may need.

7. Travel Documents:

Ensure you have all necessary travel documents, including your passport, visa (if required), travel insurance, and copies of your itineraries. It is wise to keep these documents in a secure and easily accessible place, such as a travel document organizer or a waterproof pouch.

8. Cash and Cards:

While credit and debit cards are widely accepted in Malaysia, it is always advisable to carry some cash for smaller establishments or in case of emergencies. Familiarize yourself with the local currency, the Malaysian Ringgit (MYR), and exchange some currency before your trip.

9. Electronics and Gadgets:

If you plan to capture the mesmerizing beauty of Malaysia, don't forget to pack your camera or smartphone. Additionally, consider bringing a power bank to keep your devices charged on the go.

10. Open Mind and Adventurous Spirit:

Lastly, and perhaps most importantly, pack an open mind and an adventurous spirit. Malaysia is a country rich in culture, traditions, and diverse experiences. Embrace the local customs, try new foods, and immerse yourself in the vibrant atmosphere that Malaysia has to offer.

Remember, this packing list serves as a general guide, and you may need to adjust it based on your specific needs and preferences. By packing wisely, you can ensure a hassle-free and unforgettable trip to Malaysia, where you can create memories that will last a lifetime.

Chapter 4: Geography and Climate of Malaysia

Introduction:

Welcome to the captivating landscapes and diverse climate of Malaysia. In this chapter, we will explore the physical geography of this enchanting country, from its majestic mountains and meandering rivers to its stunning coastline. Additionally, we will delve into the unique climate patterns that shape Malaysia's weather throughout the year, allowing you to prepare for an unforgettable journey. So, let's embark on this geographical and climatic adventure together!

1. The Breathtaking Terrain:

Malaysia boasts a remarkable topography that is sure to leave any nature enthusiast in awe. The country is divided into two main regions: Peninsular Malaysia and East Malaysia (comprising the states of Sabah and Sarawak). Peninsular Malaysia is primarily characterized by a mountainous backbone, known as the Main Range or Banjaran Titiwangsa, which stretches from the north to the south. Here, you will encounter peaks such as Mount Tahan, standing proudly at 2,187 meters above sea level, offering breathtaking vistas and challenging treks for adventurous souls.

2. Rivers and Lakes:

Flowing through the lush rainforests and picturesque landscapes, Malaysia's rivers are a lifeline to its diverse ecosystems. The longest river in the country is the Rajang River, which gracefully cuts through the heart of Sarawak, providing a vital water source for both wildlife and local communities. Additionally, the Kinabatangan River in Sabah offers a unique opportunity for visitors to witness the rich biodiversity of Malaysia, as it is home to numerous species of exotic birds, primates, and other wildlife.

When it comes to lakes, Malaysia is blessed with natural wonders that will leave you spellbound. One such gem is Lake Kenyir, the largest man-made lake in Southeast Asia, nestled in the state of Terengganu. Here, you can immerse yourself in tranquility, surrounded by lush rainforests, while engaging in various water activities such as fishing, kayaking, and even exploring hidden caves.

3. The Enchanting Coastline:

Malaysia's coastline stretches over 4,675 kilometers, offering a paradise for beach lovers and water enthusiasts. From the stunning white sandy beaches of Langkawi to the vibrant coral reefs of Tioman Island, there is something for everyone along this tropical coastline. The crystal-clear waters of Perhentian Islands beckon snorkelers and divers to explore its vibrant marine life, while the idyllic beaches of Penang and Malacca provide a perfect blend of history, culture, and relaxation.

4. Climate and Weather Patterns:

Malaysia's equatorial location blesses it with a tropical climate throughout the year. Expect warm and humid weather, with temperatures ranging from 25 to 35 degrees Celsius (77 to 95 degrees Fahrenheit). However, it is important to note that Malaysia experiences two distinct monsoon seasons, which significantly influence its weather patterns.

The Southwest Monsoon, also known as the Wet Monsoon, occurs from May to September, bringing heavy rainfall to the western coast of Peninsular Malaysia and parts of Sarawak. On the other hand, the Northeast Monsoon, known as the Dry Monsoon, prevails from November to March, affecting the eastern coast of Peninsular Malaysia, Sabah, and the northeastern region of Sarawak.

Conclusion:

As you plan your visit to Malaysia, understanding its geography and climate will enhance your travel experience. From exploring the majestic mountains and serene lakes to indulging in the tropical paradise of its coastline, Malaysia offers a diverse range of natural wonders. Moreover, being aware of the monsoon seasons will help you plan your activities accordingly, ensuring a comfortable and enjoyable journey. So, get ready to immerse yourself in the splendor of Malaysia's geography and embrace the warmth of its tropical climate!

Chapter 5: The Regions of Malaysia

Introduction:

Malaysia, a vibrant and diverse country in Southeast Asia, is renowned for its fascinating blend of cultures, stunning landscapes, and warm hospitality. In this chapter, we will explore the different regions of Malaysia, each with its own distinctive characteristics and attractions. From the bustling cityscapes to the tranquil rainforests, Malaysia offers a remarkable variety of experiences for every traveler.

1. Peninsular Malaysia:

The western part of Malaysia is known as Peninsular Malaysia, connected to Thailand in the north and separated from the island of Borneo by the South China Sea. This region is home to the country's capital, Kuala Lumpur, a bustling metropolis famous for its iconic Petronas Twin Towers. Peninsular Malaysia also boasts a rich historical heritage, with cities like Malacca and George Town, which are recognized as UNESCO World Heritage Sites. Visitors can explore colonial architecture, taste delicious street food, and immerse themselves in the vibrant cultural tapestry of this region.

2. East Coast:

The East Coast of Malaysia, facing the South China Sea, is a treasure trove of natural wonders. The region is renowned for its pristine beaches, crystal-clear waters, and vibrant marine life. Islands like Redang, Perhentian, and Tioman offer world-class diving and snorkeling opportunities, with colorful coral reefs teeming with exotic marine species. Besides the coastal attractions, the East Coast is also known for its traditional Malay villages, where visitors can experience the unique lifestyle and cultural traditions of the locals.

3. Borneo:

The island of Borneo, shared by Malaysia, Indonesia, and Brunei, is a paradise for nature enthusiasts. The Malaysian part of Borneo is divided into two states, Sabah and Sarawak, both offering incredible biodiversity and breathtaking landscapes. Sabah is home to Mount Kinabalu, the highest peak in Southeast Asia, and the Sepilok Orangutan Rehabilitation Centre, where visitors can witness the conservation efforts for these endangered primates. Sarawak, on the other hand, is known for its vast rainforests, diverse wildlife, and the famous Mulu Caves, a UNESCO World Heritage Site.

4. Highlands:

Escape the tropical heat and head to the Highlands of Malaysia, where cool temperatures and stunning landscapes await. The Cameron Highlands, located in Peninsular Malaysia, offer lush tea plantations, strawberry farms, and picturesque hiking trails. This region is famous for its tea production, and visitors can take a tour of the tea factories and enjoy a refreshing cup of locally produced tea. Another popular highland destination is Genting Highlands, a hill resort with a vibrant entertainment scene, including a world-class casino and theme parks.

Conclusion:

Malaysia's diverse regions offer a wealth of experiences for travelers seeking adventure, culture, and natural beauty. From the bustling city life of Kuala Lumpur to the tranquil rainforests of Borneo, each region has its own unique characteristics that make Malaysia a truly captivating destination. Whether you're exploring historical sites, diving into vibrant coral reefs, or immersing yourself in the rich cultural heritage, Malaysia promises an unforgettable journey filled with charm and authenticity.

Chapter 6: A Tapestry of History and Culture: Malaysia's Journey Through Time

Introduction:

Embark on a captivating journey through time as we delve into the rich tapestry of Malaysia's history and culture. From the earliest inhabitants to the present day, Malaysia's story is one of diversity, resilience, and the harmonious blending of various influences. In this chapter, we will explore significant events, key historical figures, and iconic sites that have shaped the nation into what it is today.

1. The Early Inhabitants:

Malaysia's history dates back thousands of years, with evidence of human presence as early as 40,000 years ago. The indigenous tribes, such as the Orang Asli and the Dayak, have inhabited these lands for generations, preserving their unique traditions and way of life. Their deep connection with nature and spiritual beliefs continue to be an integral part of Malaysia's cultural heritage.

2. The Rise of Kingdoms:

Throughout history, Malaysia has been home to various powerful kingdoms. One of the most prominent was the Malacca Sultanate, which flourished from the 15th to the 16th century. Under the rule of Sultan Mansur Shah, Malacca became a prosperous trading hub, attracting merchants from China, India, and the Middle East. The remnants of this glorious era can still be witnessed in the historic city of Malacca, a UNESCO World Heritage Site.

3. Colonial Era:

The arrival of European powers in the 16th century marked a significant turning point in Malaysia's history. The Portuguese, Dutch, and British all left their indelible marks on the nation. The British, in particular, established their presence through the formation of the

Straits Settlements, which included Penang, Malacca, and Singapore. The influence of British colonial rule can be seen in Malaysia's legal system, education, and administrative structure.

4. Independence and Modern Malaysia:

After years of struggle and determination, Malaysia gained independence from British colonial rule on August 31, 1957. Tunku Abdul Rahman, fondly known as the Father of Independence, led the nation into a new era of self-governance. Today, Malaysia stands as a testament to its multicultural society, with Malays, Chinese, Indians, and various ethnic groups coexisting harmoniously.

5. Cultural Diversity:

Malaysia's cultural landscape is a vibrant tapestry woven with diverse traditions and customs. The Malays, with their rich heritage of music, dance, and cuisine, form the majority of the population. The Chinese community, known for their vibrant festivals such as Chinese New Year, Dragon Boat Festival, and Mooncake Festival, contribute significantly to Malaysia's cultural mosaic. Meanwhile, the Indians, with their colorful celebrations like Deepavali and Thaipusam, add further depth to the nation's cultural fabric.

6. Historical Sites and Landmarks:

Malaysia boasts numerous historical sites and landmarks that offer glimpses into its past. The iconic Petronas Twin Towers in Kuala Lumpur symbolize the nation's modernity and progress, while the majestic A'Famosa fortress in Malacca takes us back to the days of Portuguese colonization. The ancient archaeological site of Lembah Bujang showcases the remnants of an ancient Hindu-Buddhist kingdom, providing insights into Malaysia's early civilization.

Conclusion:

As we conclude this chapter on Malaysia's history and culture, we are left with a profound appreciation for the nation's diverse heritage and the resilience of its people. From the earliest inhabitants to the present day, Malaysia continues to embrace its multicultural identity, fostering unity and celebrating its rich tapestry of traditions. Join us as we further explore the wonders that await in this enchanting land of history and culture.

Chapter 7: Language and People of Malaysia

Introduction:

Malaysia is a diverse country with a rich cultural heritage, influenced by various ethnic groups such as Malays, Chinese, Indians, and indigenous tribes. This diversity is reflected in the languages spoken and the social customs practiced throughout the country. In this chapter, we will provide a brief overview of the languages spoken in Malaysia, some common phrases to help you navigate your way, and essential language tips for travelers. Additionally, we will explore the social customs and etiquette that will ensure you have a pleasant and respectful experience during your visit.

Languages Spoken in Malaysia:

Malaysia is a multilingual country with Bahasa Malaysia (Malay) being the official language. However, English is widely spoken, especially in urban areas and tourist destinations. Apart from these two, Chinese dialects such as Mandarin, Cantonese, and Hokkien are also commonly spoken, particularly among the Chinese community. Tamil, a Dravidian language, is spoken by the Indian community. Additionally, various indigenous languages are spoken by the native tribes in rural areas.

Useful Phrases:

To facilitate your communication while traveling in Malaysia, here are some common phrases in Bahasa Malaysia:

1. Hello - Selamat pagi (Good morning), Selamat petang (Good afternoon/evening)

2. Thank you - Terima kasih

3. Excuse me - Maafkan saya

4. How much does it cost? - Berapa harganya?

5. Where is the restroom? - Di mana tandasnya?

6. I need help - Saya perlukan bantuan

7. Delicious - Sedap

8. Can you speak English? - Bolehkah anda berbahasa Inggeris?

9. I don't understand - Saya tidak faham

10. Goodbye - Selamat tinggal

Language Tips for Travelers:

1. Learn a few basic phrases in Bahasa Malaysia to show respect and make your interactions more enjoyable.

2. English is widely understood, but it is always helpful to carry a pocket dictionary or translation app.

3. When conversing with locals, speak slowly and clearly, as this will aid understanding.

4. Be patient and understanding if there are language barriers, and try to find alternative ways to communicate, such as gestures or pointing.

Social Customs and Etiquette:

1. Malaysians are generally polite and friendly. It is customary to greet people with a smile and a handshake.

2. When visiting someone's home, it is polite to remove your shoes before entering, unless otherwise indicated.

3. Malaysians have a diverse religious background, so it is important to respect different beliefs and practices.

4. Dress modestly, especially when visiting religious sites or rural areas, to show respect for local customs and traditions.

5. It is customary to use your right hand for eating, giving and receiving items, and shaking hands, as the left hand is considered unclean.

Conclusion:

Understanding the languages spoken in Malaysia, learning a few key phrases, and adhering to social customs and etiquette will greatly enhance your experience as a traveler. Malaysians appreciate visitors who make an effort to embrace their culture and language. By immersing yourself in the local customs, you will not only have a more authentic experience but also foster meaningful connections with the people you encounter.

Chapter 8: Traditional Cuisine of Malaysia

Introduction:

Malaysia is a country that boasts a rich and diverse culinary heritage. With influences from Malay, Chinese, Indian, and indigenous cultures, Malaysian cuisine is a delightful fusion of flavors, spices, and techniques. In this chapter, we will explore the traditional cuisine of Malaysia, highlighting its most popular dishes and ingredients. We will also provide insights on where to find the best food in the country, along with cooking tips and authentic recipes for those who wish to recreate the flavors of Malaysia in their own kitchens.

1. Malay Cuisine:

The Malay cuisine forms the foundation of traditional Malaysian food. Known for its vibrant flavors and aromatic spices, Malay dishes often feature a harmonious blend of sweet, sour, and spicy elements. Some iconic Malay dishes include Nasi Lemak (fragrant coconut rice served with sambal, fried anchovies, peanuts, and hard-boiled eggs), Rendang (slow-cooked beef or chicken in a rich coconut and spice gravy), and Satay (grilled skewered meat served with peanut sauce).

2. Chinese Cuisine:

Chinese influence on Malaysian cuisine is undeniable, especially in the bustling cities. The Chinese community in Malaysia has adapted their traditional dishes to incorporate local ingredients and flavors. Some popular Chinese-Malaysian dishes include Char Kway Teow (stir-fried flat rice noodles with prawns, bean sprouts, and soy sauce), Hainanese Chicken Rice (poached chicken served with fragrant rice and chili sauce), and Hokkien Mee (stir-fried noodles with prawns, pork, and dark soy sauce).

3. Indian Cuisine:

The Indian community in Malaysia has brought their vibrant and aromatic cuisine to the country, adding a unique dimension to the culinary scene. Indian-Malaysian dishes are known for their generous use of spices and flavors. Some must-try Indian-Malaysian dishes include Roti Canai (flaky flatbread served with curry), Banana Leaf Rice (rice served on a banana leaf with various curries and condiments), and Biryani (fragrant rice cooked with spices and meat or vegetables).

4. Indigenous Cuisine:

The indigenous communities of Malaysia have their own traditional dishes, often utilizing ingredients found in the local forests and rivers. These dishes offer a glimpse into the rich cultural heritage of Malaysia. Some indigenous dishes to look out for include Pansoh Manok (chicken cooked in bamboo with lemongrass and ginger), Ikan Terubok Masin (salted and smoked terubok fish), and Nasi Kerabu (blue-colored rice served with various herbs and condiments).

Where to Find the Best Food:

To truly experience the traditional cuisine of Malaysia, one must explore the vibrant street food culture. Cities like Kuala Lumpur, Penang, and Malacca are famous for their night markets and hawker centers, where you can find a wide variety of local delicacies. Additionally, exploring local neighborhoods and seeking out family-run restaurants will often lead to hidden gems serving authentic and traditional Malaysian dishes.

Cooking Tips and Recipes:

For those who wish to recreate the flavors of Malaysia at home, we have included some traditional recipes that capture the essence of Malaysian cuisine. From the fragrant Nasi Lemak to the fiery Sambal Belacan, these recipes will guide you through the preparation of some iconic Malaysian dishes. We have also included cooking tips to help you master the art of balancing flavors and spices, ensuring an authentic taste in your homemade Malaysian meals.

Conclusion:

The traditional cuisine of Malaysia is a true reflection of its multicultural society. With its diverse flavors and vibrant dishes, Malaysian food has gained international recognition and captivated the taste buds of travelers from around the world. Exploring the various influences and regional specialties within Malaysian cuisine is an adventure in itself, offering a unique and unforgettable culinary experience. So, dive into the world of Malaysian cuisine and savor the rich tapestry of flavors that this beautiful country has to offer.

Chapter 9: Modern Cuisine of Malaysia

Introduction:

Malaysia is a melting pot of diverse cultures, and its modern cuisine reflects this rich heritage. With influences from Malay, Chinese, Indian, and indigenous traditions, Malaysia's culinary scene has evolved into a vibrant fusion of flavors and techniques. In this chapter, we will explore the most popular dishes and ingredients that define modern Malaysian cuisine. Additionally, we will guide you to the best places to experience these culinary delights and provide cooking tips and recipes for those eager to recreate the flavors of Malaysia at home.

1. The Fusion of Flavors:

Malaysia's modern cuisine is a testament to the country's multicultural society. The blending of traditional cooking methods and ingredients from various ethnic backgrounds has resulted in a unique and exciting gastronomic experience. From spicy curries to tangy sambals, each dish tells a story of Malaysia's diverse heritage.

2. Must-Try Dishes:

a) Nasi Lemak: Considered Malaysia's national dish, nasi lemak is a fragrant coconut rice dish served with a variety of accompaniments such as sambal, fried anchovies, peanuts, and boiled eggs. This breakfast staple is a perfect introduction to the flavors of Malaysia.

b) Char Kway Teow: A popular street food, char kway teow is a stir-fried noodle dish that combines flat rice noodles, prawns, cockles, bean sprouts, and Chinese sausage. The smoky aroma and rich flavors make it a favorite among locals and tourists alike.

c) Roti Canai: Influenced by Indian cuisine, roti canai is a flaky, flatbread served with a side of curry. This versatile dish can be enjoyed plain or filled with various ingredients like egg, onion, or cheese.

3. Key Ingredients:

a) Belacan: A fermented shrimp paste, belacan is a staple in Malaysian cooking. It adds a unique umami flavor and is often used in sambal, a spicy chili paste that accompanies many dishes.

b) Lemongrass: Known for its citrusy aroma, lemongrass is frequently used in Malaysian curries and soups. It imparts a refreshing and fragrant note to these dishes.

c) Pandan: Pandan leaves are commonly used in Malaysian desserts and beverages. They lend a distinct sweet and floral flavor, enhancing dishes like pandan cake and pandan-infused rice.

4. Where to Find the Best Food:

Malaysia is renowned for its street food culture, where hawker centers and food stalls offer a wide array of delectable dishes. In Kuala Lumpur, Jalan Alor and Petaling Street are popular destinations for street food enthusiasts. Penang is also a food haven, with Gurney Drive and New Lane offering an abundance of local delights.

For a more upscale dining experience, head to the capital's trendy neighborhoods like Bangsar and Damansara Heights, where you can find modern Malaysian restaurants that elevate traditional flavors with innovative techniques.

5. Cooking Tips and Recipes:

To truly experience the flavors of Malaysia, why not try your hand at cooking some authentic dishes? Here are two simple recipes to get you started:

a) Recipe: Chicken Rendang

Rendang is a rich and flavorful curry dish that originated from the Minangkabau people of Indonesia. It has become a staple in Malaysian cuisine.

Ingredients:

- 1kg chicken, cut into pieces
- 4 shallots, finely chopped
- 4 cloves of garlic, minced
- 2 lemongrass stalks, bruised

- 4 kaffir lime leaves
- 2 cups coconut milk
- 2 tablespoons vegetable oil
- 2 tablespoons kerisik (toasted grated coconut)

Instructions:

1. Heat the oil in a large pot and sauté the shallots, garlic, lemongrass, and kaffir lime leaves until fragrant.

2. Add the chicken pieces and cook until browned.

3. Pour in the coconut milk and bring to a simmer. Cook on low heat for about 1 hour or until the chicken is tender.

4. Stir in the kerisik and cook for an additional 10 minutes.

5. Serve hot with steamed rice.

b) Recipe: Cendol

Cendol is a refreshing dessert made with pandan-flavored jelly, coconut milk, shaved ice, and palm sugar syrup.

Ingredients:

- 100g rice flour
- 1 tablespoon pandan juice
- 1 tablespoon green food coloring (optional)
- 200ml coconut milk
- 100g palm sugar
- Shaved ice

Instructions:

1. In a bowl, mix the rice flour, pandan juice, and green food coloring (if using) until well combined.

2. Bring a pot of water to a boil and pass the rice flour mixture through a sieve directly into the boiling water. Stir continuously until the mixture thickens and becomes translucent.

3. Remove from heat and rinse the cooked rice flour mixture with cold water to cool it down.

4. In a small saucepan, melt the palm sugar with a little water to create a syrup.

5. To serve, place a spoonful of the cooked rice flour mixture (cendol) into a bowl or glass. Add a generous amount of shaved ice, followed by coconut milk and palm sugar syrup.

6. Mix well before enjoying this sweet and refreshing treat.

Conclusion:

Malaysia's modern cuisine is a testament to the country's cultural diversity. From the fusion of flavors to the unique ingredients, Malaysian dishes offer a delightful culinary adventure. Whether you choose to explore the vibrant street food scene or experiment with cooking these dishes at home, the modern cuisine of Malaysia is sure to leave a lasting impression on your taste buds.

Chapter 10: Drinks and Beverages of Malaysia

Introduction:

Malaysia is not only known for its vibrant culture and delicious cuisine but also for its diverse range of refreshing drinks and beverages. From traditional herbal concoctions to modern and innovative beverages, Malaysia offers a delightful array of options for both locals and tourists alike. In this chapter, we will explore some of the most popular alcoholic and non-alcoholic drinks in Malaysia, as well as where to find the best places to enjoy them.

1. Teh Tarik:

Starting off with a non-alcoholic favorite, Teh Tarik is a must-try beverage in Malaysia. Translated as pulled tea, this unique drink is made by skillfully pouring hot tea and condensed milk back and forth between two cups, creating a frothy and creamy texture. Teh Tarik is commonly enjoyed at local street stalls known as mamak stalls, where you can witness the impressive tea-pulling technique firsthand.

2. Kopi:

Coffee lovers will be pleased to discover Malaysia's rich coffee culture. Malaysians take pride in their traditional coffee, known as Kopi. Made with dark roasted beans and brewed with a unique sock-like filter, Kopi has a robust and intense flavor. Whether you prefer it black (Kopi-O), with condensed milk (Kopi Susu), or with evaporated milk (Kopi C), you can find a variety of Kopi stalls throughout the country, particularly in the old towns and cities.

3. Teh O Ais Limau:

A popular choice to beat Malaysia's tropical heat is Teh O Ais Limau, which translates to Iced Lime Tea. This refreshing beverage combines black tea, a splash of lime juice, and a generous amount of ice. The sweet and tangy flavor makes it a perfect thirst quencher, especially during hot and humid days. You can find Teh O Ais Limau at local food courts, cafes, and even street vendors.

4. Coconut Water:

For a truly tropical experience, indulge in the natural goodness of coconut water. Malaysia is abundant in coconut trees, and the locals have mastered the art of extracting the sweet and hydrating water from young coconuts. Served chilled and straight from the coconut itself, this refreshing drink is not only delicious but also packed with essential electrolytes. You can find coconut water at local markets, roadside stalls, and even beachside vendors.

5. Tiger Beer:

Moving on to alcoholic beverages, Tiger Beer is one of Malaysia's most popular choices. This lager-style beer has a crisp and refreshing taste, making it an ideal accompaniment to local dishes such as satay or nasi lemak. You can find Tiger Beer in almost every bar, pub, or restaurant across the country, as well as in convenience stores and supermarkets.

6. Tuak:

For those seeking a taste of Malaysia's indigenous culture, Tuak is a traditional rice wine made by the indigenous communities of Sarawak and Sabah. This homemade alcoholic beverage is made from fermented glutinous rice and has a sweet and slightly tangy flavor. It is often served during festive occasions and cultural ceremonies. To experience the authentic taste of Tuak, it is best to visit the longhouses in Sarawak or attend cultural festivals in Sabah.

Conclusion:

Malaysia's drinks and beverages offer a delightful blend of flavors, ranging from traditional favorites to modern innovations. Whether you prefer a refreshing non-alcoholic beverage like Teh Tarik or a local beer like Tiger Beer, Malaysia has something to satisfy every palate. So, don't miss the opportunity to explore and indulge in the diverse range of drinks and beverages that this beautiful country has to offer.

Chapter 11: Dining out in Malaysia

Introduction:

Malaysia is a gastronomic paradise, offering a diverse range of culinary delights that will leave your taste buds tingling with delight. From street food to fine dining, the country is renowned for its rich and flavorful cuisine. In this chapter, we will provide you with essential tips on how to make the most of your dining experience in Malaysia, including choosing the right restaurant, ordering food, and settling the bill. Additionally, we will recommend some exceptional restaurants in various parts of the country that are sure to satisfy your cravings.

1. Choosing the Right Restaurant:

a. Research: Before venturing out for a meal, it is advisable to conduct some research. Look for reviews, recommendations, and ratings online to ensure you choose a reputable restaurant that aligns with your preferences.

b. Local Recommendations: Seek recommendations from locals or hotel staff who are often well-versed in the best dining establishments in the area.

c. Hygiene Standards: Pay attention to cleanliness and hygiene when choosing a restaurant. Look for establishments with high sanitation ratings to ensure a safe dining experience.

2. Ordering Food:

a. Embrace Local Cuisine: Malaysia is a melting pot of cultures, and its cuisine reflects this diversity. Don't hesitate to try local dishes such as Nasi Lemak, Char Kway Teow, or Roti Canai for an authentic experience.

b. Spice Level: Malaysian cuisine is known for its bold and vibrant flavors, often accompanied by a spicy kick. If you have a low tolerance for spice, don't hesitate to request milder versions of dishes or ask for recommendations from the waitstaff.

c. Dietary Restrictions: If you have any dietary restrictions or allergies, communicate them clearly to the waitstaff to ensure your needs are accommodated.

3. Settling the Bill:

a. Tipping: Tipping is not customary in Malaysia, as a 10% service charge is usually included in the bill. However, if you receive exceptional service, a small tip would be greatly appreciated.

b. Splitting the Bill: When dining in a group, it is common to split the bill equally among all participants. Inform the waitstaff beforehand if you wish to have separate bills.

c. Payment Options: Most restaurants in Malaysia accept cash and major credit cards. However, it is advisable to carry some cash as smaller establishments or street food vendors may not accept cards.

Recommended Restaurants:

1. Kuala Lumpur:

a. Bijan Bar & Restaurant: Offering traditional Malay cuisine with a modern twist, Bijan is renowned for its elegant ambiance and impeccable service.

b. Jalan Alor: This vibrant street in Kuala Lumpur is a haven for food lovers, offering a wide variety of local street food stalls and restaurants.

2. Penang:

a. Noor & Dean's Kafe: Situated in George Town, this charming cafe serves mouthwatering Nyonya cuisine, showcasing the unique flavors of the Peranakan culture.

b. Gurney Drive Hawker Center: A must-visit for food enthusiasts, this bustling hawker center offers an array of Penang's famous street food, including Char Koay Teow and Assam Laksa.

3. Langkawi:

a. The Gulai House: Nestled amidst the lush rainforest, this open-air restaurant offers a serene dining experience with traditional Malay dishes prepared using fresh local ingredients.

b. Orkid Ria Seafood Restaurant: Located on Pantai Cenang Beach, this restaurant is renowned for its delectable seafood dishes and stunning sunset views.

Conclusion:

Dining out in Malaysia is an adventure for the senses, where you can indulge in a tapestry of flavors and experience the warmth of Malaysian hospitality. By following the tips provided in this chapter, you can make informed choices, savor the local cuisine, and create unforgettable dining memories. Remember, Malaysia's culinary scene is as diverse as its people, so be open to new experiences and let your taste buds take you on a delightful journey.

Chapter 12: Food and Drink Festivals in Malaysia

Introduction:

Malaysia is a melting pot of diverse cultures, and one of the best ways to experience this cultural fusion is through its vibrant food and drink festivals. From traditional Malay delicacies to Indian spices and Chinese street food, Malaysia offers a wide array of flavors that will tantalize your taste buds. In this chapter, we will explore the calendar of major food and drink festivals in Malaysia, providing you with an opportunity to immerse yourself in the country's rich culinary heritage.

1. Ramadan Bazaars:

Every year during the holy month of Ramadan, Malaysia comes alive with bustling Ramadan bazaars. These vibrant markets offer a wide variety of traditional Malay dishes, such as Nasi Lemak, Satay, and Roti Canai. The aroma of freshly grilled meats and the sight of colorful desserts will tempt you at every corner. Join the locals as they break their fast and experience the lively atmosphere of these bazaars.

2. George Town Festival:

Held annually in the UNESCO World Heritage Site of George Town, Penang, the George Town Festival is a celebration of art, culture, and of course, food. As part of the festival, the Street Food Festival takes center stage, showcasing Penang's renowned hawker fare. Indulge in Char Kway Teow, Assam Laksa, and Penang Rojak while enjoying live performances and art installations.

3. Malaysia International Gastronomy Festival:

For all the food connoisseurs out there, the Malaysia International Gastronomy Festival is a must-visit. This month-long celebration brings together renowned local and international chefs, who showcase their culinary expertise through exclusive menus and events. From fine dining experiences to cooking classes, this festival offers a unique opportunity to savor exquisite cuisine from around the world.

4. Rainforest World Music Festival:

While primarily a music festival, the Rainforest World Music Festival in Sarawak also boasts a diverse range of food and drink options. Experience the flavors of Borneo as you sample traditional dishes such as Manok Pansoh (chicken cooked in bamboo) and Sarawak Laksa, while enjoying the captivating sounds of world music. Immerse yourself in the cultural fusion of food and music in the heart of the Bornean rainforest.

5. Malaysia Coffee Fest:

Coffee lovers rejoice! The Malaysia Coffee Fest is a haven for caffeine enthusiasts, showcasing the best of Malaysia's coffee scene. From artisanal brews to specialty coffee beans, this festival offers a unique opportunity to taste and learn about the country's coffee culture. Attend workshops, watch latte art competitions, and discover the perfect cup of joe to suit your palate.

6. Sabah Harvest Festival:

The Sabah Harvest Festival, also known as Pesta Kaamatan, is a celebration of the indigenous Kadazan-Dusun culture in Sabah. Alongside traditional music and dance performances, this festival showcases an array of local delicacies. Indulge in dishes like Hinava (raw fish salad), Pinasakan (braised fish), and Ambuyat (sago starch) while immersing yourself in the rich cultural heritage of Sabah.

Conclusion:

Food and drink festivals in Malaysia offer a unique opportunity to explore the country's diverse culinary traditions. From the bustling Ramadan bazaars to the coffee-centric Malaysia Coffee Fest, there is something for every food lover. Immerse yourself in the vibrant flavors and cultural fusion of Malaysia as you indulge in traditional dishes and discover new culinary experiences.

Chapter 13: Getting to Malaysia

Introduction:

Malaysia, a vibrant and diverse country in Southeast Asia, is a popular destination for travelers from all around the world. To reach this enchanting land, there are several modes of transportation available, each offering a unique experience. Whether you prefer the convenience of air travel or the scenic routes offered by train, bus, car, or ferry, this chapter will guide you through the various options to help you plan your journey to Malaysia.

1. By Plane:

Malaysia is well-connected to major cities worldwide, making air travel the most convenient mode of transportation for international visitors. Kuala Lumpur International Airport (KLIA) serves as the primary gateway, offering direct flights from numerous destinations. Other major airports, such as Penang International Airport and Kota Kinabalu International Airport, also cater to international flights. With a wide range of airlines to choose from, finding a suitable flight to Malaysia is relatively easy.

2. By Train:

For those seeking a scenic and immersive journey, traveling to Malaysia by train is an excellent choice. The Keretapi Tanah Melayu Berhad (KTMB) operates train services connecting Malaysia with neighboring countries like Thailand and Singapore. The Eastern & Oriental Express, a luxurious train service, is another option for travelers seeking a unique and indulgent experience. These train journeys offer breathtaking views of lush landscapes, picturesque towns, and cultural landmarks, allowing you to truly appreciate the beauty of Southeast Asia.

3. By Bus:

Traveling to Malaysia by bus is a cost-effective option, especially for those coming from neighboring countries. An extensive network of bus routes connects Malaysia with Thailand, Singapore, and other nearby destinations. Buses are a popular choice for backpackers and budget travelers, as they provide an affordable and flexible means of transportation. With comfortable seating and regular departures, bus travel offers convenience and the opportunity to explore the scenic countryside along the way.

4. By Car:

For travelers who prefer the freedom of the open road, driving to Malaysia can be an exciting adventure. Malaysia is well-connected by an extensive network of highways, making it easily accessible from neighboring countries. However, it is important to familiarize yourself with the local traffic rules and regulations. Cross-border driving may require additional documentation, such as an international driving permit, so be sure to check the requirements beforehand. Driving through Malaysia allows you to explore at your own pace, uncover hidden gems, and immerse yourself in the country's diverse landscapes.

5. By Ferry:

If you are planning to visit the beautiful islands of Malaysia, such as Langkawi or Tioman, traveling by ferry is the most convenient option. Several ferry services operate between Malaysia and neighboring countries like Thailand and Indonesia. These ferry rides offer breathtaking views of the crystal-clear waters, lush greenery, and stunning coastlines. Whether you are a beach lover or an adventure enthusiast, traveling by ferry adds an element of excitement to your journey.

Conclusion:

Getting to Malaysia is an adventure in itself, with various modes of transportation to suit every traveler's preferences. Whether you choose to fly, take a train, hop on a bus, drive, or sail by ferry, each option provides a unique experience and an opportunity to explore the diverse landscapes and cultures of Malaysia. Plan your journey wisely, considering factors such as time, budget, and personal preferences, to ensure a smooth and enjoyable trip to this captivating country.

Chapter 14: Getting Around by Public Transportation in Malaysia

Introduction:

Welcome to Chapter 14 of our tourist guide, where we will explore the various modes of public transportation available in Malaysia. Whether you're a budget traveler or simply want to experience the local way of getting around, Malaysia offers a reliable and efficient public transportation system that includes trains, buses, and metros. In this chapter, we will provide you with an overview of each mode of transportation and a map of the public transportation system in the capital city.

1. Trains:

Malaysia boasts an extensive railway network that connects major cities and towns across the country. The two main train systems are the KTM (Keretapi Tanah Melayu) and the LRT (Light Rail Transit). The KTM offers intercity and interstate services, making it an excellent option for long-distance travel. On the other hand, the LRT operates within the city, providing convenient access to popular tourist spots and residential areas.

2. Buses:

Buses are a popular mode of transportation in Malaysia due to their affordability and extensive coverage. The country has a well-established bus network that connects even the most remote areas. RapidKL is the main bus operator in Kuala Lumpur, offering both local and express services. Additionally, there are several long-distance bus companies that provide connections between major cities, making it an ideal choice for travelers exploring different regions of Malaysia.

3. Metros:

If you're visiting the capital city of Kuala Lumpur, you'll have the opportunity to experience the efficient metro system known as the MRT (Mass Rapid Transit). The MRT covers various routes within the city, including popular tourist destinations, shopping districts, and residential areas. With its air-conditioned carriages and frequent services, the MRT offers a comfortable and convenient way to navigate Kuala Lumpur.

Map of the Public Transportation System in Kuala Lumpur:

To help you navigate the public transportation system in Kuala Lumpur, we have included a map that showcases the train lines, bus routes, and metro stations. This comprehensive map will assist you in planning your journeys and identifying the best routes to reach your desired destinations. Remember to refer to this map whenever you're exploring the city, as it will undoubtedly make your travel experience more enjoyable and hassle-free.

Conclusion:

As you can see, Malaysia offers a diverse range of public transportation options, including trains, buses, and metros. Whether you're traveling within the city or exploring different regions, these modes of transportation will ensure that you can easily reach your desired destinations. With the provided map, you'll have no trouble navigating Kuala Lumpur's public transportation system and making the most of your time in Malaysia. Enjoy the convenience, affordability, and efficiency of Malaysia's public transportation as you explore this beautiful country.

Chapter 15: Types of Accommodation in Malaysia

Introduction:

Malaysia, a vibrant and diverse country, offers an array of accommodation options to suit every traveler's preference and budget. From luxurious hotels to cozy guesthouses and unique Airbnbs, this chapter will guide you through the different types of accommodation available in Malaysia, ensuring you find the perfect place to stay during your visit.

1. Hotels:

Malaysia boasts a wide range of hotels, catering to various budgets and needs. From world-class luxury hotels in the heart of Kuala Lumpur to charming boutique hotels in Penang's heritage neighborhoods, you'll find accommodation options that provide exceptional service and amenities. Whether you seek a lavish experience or a comfortable stay, hotels in Malaysia offer a diverse range of choices.

2. Hostels:

Ideal for budget-conscious travelers, hostels are a popular choice among backpackers and solo adventurers. Malaysia has numerous hostels scattered across major cities and tourist destinations. These budget-friendly accommodations provide dormitory-style rooms or private rooms at affordable rates. Hostels often offer communal spaces, allowing guests to socialize and connect with fellow travelers from around the world.

3. Guesthouses:

For those seeking a more intimate and homely experience, guesthouses in Malaysia are an excellent choice. Found in both urban and rural areas, guesthouses provide cozy rooms and personalized service. Many guesthouses are family-run, giving guests a chance to immerse themselves in Malaysian culture and hospitality. These accommodations are often located in charming neighborhoods, providing a unique and authentic experience.

4. Airbnbs:

In recent years, the popularity of Airbnb has grown significantly in Malaysia. With a wide range of options available, travelers can choose from entire apartments, private rooms, or unique accommodations such as traditional Malay houses or colonial bungalows. Staying in an Airbnb allows you to experience local neighborhoods and interact with friendly hosts who can provide insider tips and recommendations.

5. Resorts:

Malaysia is renowned for its breathtaking beaches and lush rainforests, making it an ideal destination for resort enthusiasts. The country offers a multitude of beach resorts, jungle retreats, and eco-lodges. These accommodations provide a serene and tranquil environment, often surrounded by stunning natural landscapes. Resorts in Malaysia offer a plethora of amenities, including spa facilities, water sports, and guided nature tours.

Conclusion:

When planning your trip to Malaysia, the accommodation options are plentiful and diverse. Whether you prefer the lavishness of a hotel, the social atmosphere of a hostel, the warmth of a guesthouse, the uniqueness of an Airbnb, or the tranquility of a resort, Malaysia has something for everyone. By understanding the different types of accommodation available, you can choose the perfect place to stay and enhance your overall travel experience in this beautiful Southeast Asian nation.

Chapter 16: Tips for Staying in Malaysia

Introduction:

Welcome to Malaysia, a vibrant and diverse country that offers a plethora of cultural experiences, delicious cuisine, and breathtaking landscapes. To ensure a smooth and enjoyable stay, it is essential to be well-prepared and knowledgeable about certain aspects of Malaysian culture and lifestyle. In this chapter, we will provide you with valuable tips for booking accommodation, getting around, and staying safe during your visit to Malaysia.

Booking Accommodation:

1. Research and Compare: Before making any reservations, take the time to research and compare different accommodations. Consider factors such as location, amenities, and reviews from previous guests to find the perfect fit for your needs and preferences.

2. Book in Advance: Malaysia is a popular tourist destination, so it is advisable to book your accommodation in advance, especially during peak seasons or major events. This will ensure you have a wider range of options and avoid last-minute disappointments.

3. Consider Homestays: If you want a more immersive cultural experience, consider staying in a homestay. This will allow you to live with a local family, learn about their customs, and indulge in authentic Malaysian hospitality.

Getting Around:

1. Public Transportation: Malaysia has an efficient public transportation system, including buses, trains, and monorails. Utilize these options to explore different cities and save on transportation costs. Purchase a Touch 'n Go card for convenient access to various modes of public transport.

2. Ride-Hailing Apps: Grab and other ride-hailing apps are widely used in Malaysia. They provide a convenient and affordable way to get

around, especially for shorter distances or when public transportation is less accessible.

3. Renting a Car: If you plan to venture outside major cities or prefer more flexibility, renting a car can be a good option. Ensure you have an international driving license, familiarize yourself with local traffic rules, and consider the availability of parking spaces.

Staying Safe:

1. Respect Local Customs: Malaysia is a multicultural country with diverse religious and cultural practices. Respect local customs, dress modestly when visiting religious sites, and be mindful of local sensitivities to avoid any misunderstandings.

2. Stay Alert: While Malaysia is generally safe for tourists, it is always wise to stay alert and aware of your surroundings. Keep an eye on your belongings, avoid isolated areas at night, and be cautious when interacting with strangers.

3. Emergency Numbers: Familiarize yourself with Malaysia's emergency contact numbers, including the police (999), ambulance (999), and tourist police (03-2149 6590). Keep these numbers handy in case of any unforeseen circumstances.

Conclusion:

By following these tips, you can enhance your experience of staying in Malaysia and make the most of your visit. Remember to plan ahead, respect local customs, and prioritize your safety. Malaysia welcomes you with open arms, ready to offer unforgettable memories and warm hospitality. Enjoy your stay and embrace the wonders this remarkable country has to offer.

Chapter 17: Must-see Attractions in Malaysia

Introduction:

Welcome to Malaysia, a captivating Southeast Asian destination that boasts a rich cultural heritage, stunning natural landscapes, and a melting pot of diverse influences. In this chapter, we will explore the top 10 must-see attractions in Malaysia, each offering a unique experience that will leave you in awe.

1. Petronas Twin Towers, Kuala Lumpur:

Standing tall in the heart of Kuala Lumpur, the Petronas Twin Towers are an iconic symbol of Malaysia's modernity. Soaring 452 meters into the sky, these twin skyscrapers offer breathtaking views from the observation deck, a world-class shopping experience at Suria KLCC, and an opportunity to witness the mesmerizing Symphony Lake musical fountain show at night.

2. Mount Kinabalu, Sabah:

Nature enthusiasts and adventure seekers should not miss the opportunity to conquer Mount Kinabalu, the highest peak in Southeast Asia. This majestic mountain offers a challenging yet rewarding climb, surrounded by lush rainforests and breathtaking vistas. The experience of witnessing the sunrise from the summit is truly unforgettable.

3. George Town, Penang:

Listed as a UNESCO World Heritage Site, George Town is a vibrant city that showcases Malaysia's multicultural heritage. Stroll through its narrow streets, adorned with colorful colonial buildings, and discover the famous street art that has become a hallmark of the city. Indulge in the diverse street food scene, visit historic temples, and immerse yourself in the unique blend of cultures that make George Town so special.

4. Langkawi Island, Kedah:

Escape to the tropical paradise of Langkawi, an archipelago of 99 islands surrounded by turquoise waters. With pristine beaches, lush rainforests, and stunning waterfalls, Langkawi offers a perfect blend of relaxation and adventure. Explore the mangrove forests, take a cable car ride to the top of Mount Mat Cincang, and witness the magical beauty of the Seven Wells Waterfall.

5. Malacca City, Malacca:

Step back in time as you explore the historic city of Malacca, a UNESCO World Heritage Site. Immerse yourself in the rich history and cultural heritage of Malaysia as you wander through the well-preserved colonial buildings, visit ancient temples, and explore the vibrant Jonker Street night market. Don't forget to try the famous Nyonya cuisine, a fusion of Chinese and Malay flavors.

6. Borneo Rainforest, Sarawak:

Embark on a journey into the heart of Borneo's ancient rainforest, a biodiversity hotspot that is home to unique flora and fauna, including the endangered orangutans. Explore the national parks of Sarawak, such as Bako National Park and Gunung Mulu National Park, where you can witness stunning caves, towering limestone pinnacles, and a diverse range of wildlife.

7. Cameron Highlands, Pahang:

Escape the heat and immerse yourself in the cool climate of the Cameron Highlands. This picturesque hill station is renowned for its tea plantations, strawberry farms, and scenic hiking trails. Take a leisurely stroll through the tea estates, visit the iconic BOH Tea Plantation, and indulge in a traditional English afternoon tea experience.

8. Taman Negara National Park, Pahang:

Discover one of the oldest rainforests in the world at Taman Negara National Park. This vast wilderness offers an abundance of wildlife, thrilling jungle treks, and the opportunity to experience the local indigenous cultures. Embark on a river safari, trek through the canopy walkway, and witness the mesmerizing beauty of the nocturnal creatures.

9. Perhentian Islands, Terengganu:

For those seeking a tropical island getaway, the Perhentian Islands are a must-visit destination. With crystal-clear waters, vibrant coral reefs, and white sandy beaches, these islands offer a paradise for snorkeling and diving enthusiasts. Immerse yourself in the laid-back island life, unwind on the pristine beaches, and swim alongside colorful marine life.

10. Batu Caves, Selangor:

A visit to Malaysia would not be complete without exploring the iconic Batu Caves. Located just outside Kuala Lumpur, these limestone caves are a significant Hindu shrine and a popular tourist attraction. Climb the 272 steps to reach the main cave, marvel at the towering golden statue of Lord Murugan, and witness the vibrant Thaipusam festival if you visit during the right time.

Conclusion:

Malaysia offers a plethora of must-see attractions that cater to every traveler's interests. From modern architectural marvels to ancient rainforests, cultural heritage sites to pristine islands, this diverse country has something for everyone. Embark on a journey of discovery and let Malaysia's beauty and charm captivate your senses.

Chapter 18: Natural Wonders of Malaysia

Introduction:

Malaysia is a country blessed with an abundance of natural wonders that will leave any traveler in awe. From stunning rainforests to breathtaking islands, Malaysia offers a diverse range of landscapes and ecosystems that are truly unique. In this chapter, we will explore the top 10 natural wonders of Malaysia, each offering a distinct experience that showcases the country's rich biodiversity and natural beauty.

1. Taman Negara National Park:

Taman Negara National Park is one of the oldest rainforests in the world, dating back over 130 million years. This vast expanse of dense forest is home to an incredible array of flora and fauna, including endangered species such as the Malayan tiger and Asian elephant. Visitors can explore the park through guided treks, river cruises, and canopy walks, immersing themselves in the untouched beauty of this ancient rainforest.

2. Mount Kinabalu:

Rising majestically in Sabah, Mount Kinabalu is the highest peak in Southeast Asia, standing at 4,095 meters. This UNESCO World Heritage Site is not only a challenging climb for adventure enthusiasts but also a haven for unique plant species, including the famous Rafflesia flower. The panoramic views from the summit and the surrounding Kinabalu National Park make this natural wonder a must-visit for nature lovers.

3. Langkawi Geopark:

Located in the Andaman Sea, Langkawi Geopark is a geological marvel comprising 99 islands. This UNESCO Global Geopark offers stunning landscapes, including limestone formations, caves, and pristine beaches. Visitors can take boat tours, hike through the rainforest, or explore the mangroves, witnessing the rich biodiversity and geological wonders that make Langkawi a true natural gem.

4. Borneo Rainforest:

The Borneo Rainforest, shared by Malaysia, Indonesia, and Brunei, is the oldest rainforest in the world and a biodiversity hotspot. This vast ecosystem is home to unique wildlife, such as orangutans, proboscis monkeys, and pygmy elephants. Exploring the dense jungle, cruising down the Kinabatangan River, or visiting the Sepilok Orangutan Rehabilitation Centre are just a few ways to experience the wonders of this ancient rainforest.

5. Perhentian Islands:

Situated off the coast of northeastern Malaysia, the Perhentian Islands are a tropical paradise renowned for their crystal-clear waters and vibrant coral reefs. Snorkeling or diving in these pristine waters will reveal a kaleidoscope of marine life, including turtles, reef sharks, and colorful coral formations. With its untouched beauty and laid-back atmosphere, the Perhentian Islands are a haven for beach lovers and underwater enthusiasts.

6. Cameron Highlands:

Nestled in the Titiwangsa Range, the Cameron Highlands is a cool retreat known for its tea plantations, strawberry farms, and lush green landscapes. The region's unique climate and fertile soil create the perfect conditions for cultivating tea, flowers, and vegetables. Visitors can explore the tea estates, hike through mossy forests, and indulge in the cool mountain air while enjoying the breathtaking vistas of the highlands.

7. Gunung Mulu National Park:

Gunung Mulu National Park, a UNESCO World Heritage Site, is a treasure trove of natural wonders. The park is home to the world's largest cave chamber, the Sarawak Chamber, and numerous other impressive caves, such as the Deer Cave and Clearwater Cave. The park's diverse ecosystems also support a wide range of flora and fauna, making it a paradise for nature enthusiasts and spelunkers alike.

8. Tioman Island:

Tioman Island, located off the east coast of Peninsular Malaysia, is a tropical paradise renowned for its pristine beaches, crystal-clear waters, and vibrant coral reefs. This idyllic island offers a range of activities, including snorkeling, diving, jungle trekking, and relaxing on secluded beaches. With its lush rainforest and abundant marine life, Tioman Island is a natural wonder that captivates visitors with its beauty.

9. Kinabalu Park:

Kinabalu Park, a UNESCO World Heritage Site, is a botanical paradise nestled around Mount Kinabalu. This park boasts an incredible diversity of plant species, including the pitcher plant and orchids, making it a paradise for botanists and nature lovers. The park also offers various hiking trails, hot springs, and stunning vistas, allowing visitors to immerse themselves in the natural wonders of this unique ecosystem.

10. Belum-Temengor Rainforest:

Belum-Temengor Rainforest, located in northern Peninsular Malaysia, is one of the oldest rainforests in the world and a sanctuary for endangered species. This vast wilderness is home to the elusive Malayan tiger, Asian elephant, and tapir, among others. Visitors can explore the rainforest through boat cruises, jungle treks, and wildlife spotting, experiencing the untouched beauty and remarkable biodiversity of this natural wonder.

Conclusion:

Malaysia's natural wonders offer a captivating blend of ancient rainforests, pristine islands, and unique ecosystems that showcase the country's remarkable biodiversity. From the majestic Mount Kinabalu to the untouched beauty of Taman Negara, each natural wonder provides a unique experience for travelers seeking to connect with nature. By preserving these treasures and promoting sustainable tourism, Malaysia ensures that future generations can continue to marvel at the country's natural wonders.

Chapter 19: Historical and Cultural Sites in Malaysia

Introduction:

Malaysia is a country rich in history and culture, with a diverse heritage that reflects its unique blend of Malay, Chinese, Indian, and indigenous influences. This chapter will take you on a journey through Malaysia's top 10 historical and cultural sites, each offering a glimpse into the country's fascinating past and vibrant present.

1. Malacca Historic City, Malacca:

Known as the Historic State, Malacca is a UNESCO World Heritage Site and a living testament to Malaysia's colonial past. Explore the well-preserved Dutch architecture, visit the iconic Stadthuys, and stroll along Jonker Street, famous for its antique shops and vibrant night market.

2. Georgetown, Penang:

Another UNESCO World Heritage Site, Georgetown is a treasure trove of historical and cultural landmarks. Marvel at the colorful street art, visit the Khoo Kongsi clan house, and explore the captivating Peranakan heritage at the Pinang Peranakan Mansion.

3. Kuching Old Town, Sarawak:

Nestled on the banks of the Sarawak River, Kuching Old Town boasts a rich history influenced by the Brooke dynasty. Immerse yourself in the city's colonial charm, visit the Sarawak Museum, and take a leisurely walk along the picturesque waterfront.

4. Taman Negara, Pahang:

For a taste of Malaysia's natural and cultural heritage, head to Taman Negara, the oldest rainforest in the world. Embark on a thrilling jungle trek, interact with indigenous tribes, and learn about their traditional way of life.

5. Batu Caves, Selangor:

A significant Hindu religious site, the Batu Caves are a series of limestone caves and cave temples. Climb the 272 steps to the main cave and marvel at the towering statue of Lord Murugan. Don't miss the annual Thaipusam festival, where devotees perform various rituals and processions.

6. Kota Kinabalu, Sabah:

While Kota Kinabalu is renowned for its stunning natural beauty, it also offers a glimpse into Sabah's cultural heritage. Explore the Mari Mari Cultural Village, where you can experience traditional dances, crafts, and the unique lifestyle of the indigenous tribes.

7. Sultan Abdul Samad Building, Kuala Lumpur:

Standing proudly in the heart of Kuala Lumpur, the Sultan Abdul Samad Building is an iconic symbol of Malaysia's colonial past. Admire the stunning Moorish architecture and learn about its historical significance as the former British administrative center.

8. St. Paul's Church, Melaka:

Perched on St. Paul's Hill, this church is one of the oldest surviving Christian buildings in Malaysia. Explore the ruins, visit the nearby A Famosa fortress, and enjoy panoramic views of Malacca from the hilltop.

9. Sarawak Cultural Village, Sarawak:

Immerse yourself in Sarawak's diverse cultural heritage at the Sarawak Cultural Village. Discover traditional longhouses, witness cultural performances, and learn about the customs and traditions of the various indigenous tribes.

10. Islamic Arts Museum, Kuala Lumpur:

Located in the heart of the city, the Islamic Arts Museum houses an impressive collection of Islamic art from around the world. Explore the exhibits showcasing calligraphy, textiles, ceramics, and architecture, and gain a deeper understanding of Islamic culture.

Conclusion:

Malaysia's historical and cultural sites offer a captivating journey through time, allowing visitors to appreciate the country's rich heritage. From colonial architecture to ancient rainforests and indigenous traditions, these top 10 sites provide a unique and truthful glimpse into Malaysia's diverse past and vibrant present.

Chapter 20: Museums and Art Galleries in Malaysia

Introduction:

Malaysia is a country rich in cultural heritage and artistic expression. From ancient artifacts to contemporary masterpieces, the museums and art galleries in Malaysia offer a fascinating journey through the country's diverse history and artistic traditions. In this chapter, we will explore the top 10 museums and art galleries that are not to be missed during your visit to Malaysia.

1. National Museum, Kuala Lumpur:

Located in the heart of Kuala Lumpur, the National Museum is a treasure trove of Malaysian history. Its collection includes ancient artifacts, traditional costumes, and historical documents that showcase the country's rich heritage. The museum's interactive exhibits and informative displays provide visitors with a comprehensive understanding of Malaysia's past.

2. Islamic Arts Museum, Kuala Lumpur:

Dedicated to Islamic art and culture, the Islamic Arts Museum in Kuala Lumpur is a true architectural gem. Its collection features intricate calligraphy, exquisite ceramics, and stunning textiles from various Islamic civilizations. The museum's serene atmosphere and beautifully curated galleries offer a unique insight into the Islamic world.

3. Penang State Museum and Art Gallery, George Town:

Situated in the UNESCO World Heritage Site of George Town, the Penang State Museum and Art Gallery is a must-visit for art enthusiasts. Its extensive collection includes contemporary artworks, historical artifacts, and traditional crafts that reflect the multicultural heritage of Penang. The museum also hosts temporary exhibitions, showcasing the works of local and international artists.

4. Sarawak Cultural Village, Kuching:

For a glimpse into the indigenous cultures of Malaysia, a visit to the Sarawak Cultural Village in Kuching is highly recommended. This living museum showcases traditional longhouses, handicraft demonstrations, and cultural performances by the various ethnic groups of Sarawak. The immersive experience allows visitors to learn about the unique traditions and customs of the indigenous communities.

5. National Visual Arts Gallery, Kuala Lumpur:

As the premier art institution in Malaysia, the National Visual Arts Gallery is a haven for contemporary art lovers. Its extensive collection features paintings, sculptures, and installations by renowned Malaysian artists. The gallery also hosts regular exhibitions, workshops, and art events, making it a vibrant hub for the local art scene.

6. Peranakan Museum, Malacca:

Located in the historic city of Malacca, the Peranakan Museum offers a fascinating insight into the Peranakan culture. The museum showcases the unique heritage of the Peranakan community through its collection of traditional costumes, porcelain, and furniture. Visitors can also learn about the customs, traditions, and cuisine of the Peranakan people.

7. Sabah Art Gallery, Kota Kinabalu:

Nestled amidst lush greenery in Kota Kinabalu, the Sabah Art Gallery is dedicated to promoting local Sabahan artists. The gallery features a diverse range of artworks, including paintings, sculptures, and photography, that reflect the beauty and diversity of Sabah. Visitors can also participate in art workshops and events organized by the gallery.

8. Muzium Negara, Penang:

Situated in the charming town of Penang, the Muzium Negara is a hidden gem that showcases the history and culture of the state. Its collection includes historical artifacts, traditional costumes, and archival photographs that depict the journey of Penang from its early days to the present. The museum's well-curated exhibits provide a captivating narrative of Penang's past.

9. Pahang Art Museum, Kuantan:

Nestled in the capital city of Pahang, the Pahang Art Museum is a haven for art enthusiasts. The museum's collection features a wide range of artworks, including paintings, sculptures, and installations, by local and international artists. The museum also hosts art workshops and exhibitions, providing a platform for emerging artists to showcase their talent.

10. Taiping War Cemetery and Museum, Taiping:

The Taiping War Cemetery and Museum is a solemn reminder of Malaysia's wartime history. The museum displays artifacts, photographs, and personal stories that commemorate the fallen soldiers from World War II. The beautifully maintained cemetery is a peaceful place for reflection and pays tribute to those who sacrificed their lives.

Conclusion:

The museums and art galleries in Malaysia offer a captivating journey through the country's rich history, diverse cultures, and vibrant art scene. From ancient artifacts to contemporary masterpieces, these institutions provide a unique and truthful insight into Malaysia's heritage and artistic expression. A visit to these top 10 museums and art galleries is sure to leave you with a deeper appreciation for Malaysia's cultural tapestry.

Chapter 21: Religious Sites in Malaysia

Introduction:

Malaysia is a country known for its rich cultural diversity and religious harmony. With a population comprising of various ethnicities and religions, Malaysia is home to a wide array of religious sites that hold great significance for locals and tourists alike. In this chapter, we will explore the top 10 religious sites in Malaysia, each offering a unique glimpse into the country's religious tapestry.

1. Batu Caves, Selangor:

Located just outside of Kuala Lumpur, the Batu Caves are a prominent Hindu shrine in Malaysia. The main attraction is the towering limestone hill, which houses a series of caves adorned with colorful Hindu statues and idols. The annual Thaipusam festival attracts thousands of devotees who come to pay homage and fulfill their vows.

2. Masjid Negara, Kuala Lumpur:

Also known as the National Mosque, Masjid Negara is an iconic symbol of Islam in Malaysia. Its modernist design and impressive architecture make it one of the most visited religious sites in the country. Visitors can explore the grand prayer hall, beautiful gardens, and learn about the Islamic faith through guided tours.

3. Kek Lok Si Temple, Penang:

Situated in the hills of Air Itam, the Kek Lok Si Temple is the largest Buddhist temple in Southeast Asia. This sprawling complex features a stunning seven-tiered pagoda, numerous prayer halls, and a towering statue of the Goddess of Mercy. The temple offers breathtaking panoramic views of Penang Island, making it a must-visit for both spiritual seekers and nature enthusiasts.

4. St. Paul's Church, Melaka:

Steeped in history, St. Paul's Church in Melaka stands as a testament to Malaysia's colonial past. Built by the Portuguese in the

16th century, this church was later converted into a burial ground for Dutch nobility. Today, visitors can explore the ruins, admire the beautiful frescoes, and enjoy panoramic views of the city from the hilltop location.

5. Sri Mahamariamman Temple, Kuala Lumpur:

Nestled in the heart of Kuala Lumpur's vibrant Chinatown, the Sri Mahamariamman Temple is the oldest Hindu temple in the city. Its intricate façade, adorned with vibrant sculptures and colorful motifs, is a sight to behold. Step inside to witness the rituals and ceremonies that take place, immersing yourself in the rich Hindu culture.

6. Cheng Hoon Teng Temple, Melaka:

Regarded as the oldest Chinese temple in Malaysia, Cheng Hoon Teng Temple is a captivating blend of Taoism, Confucianism, and Buddhism. Its ornate architecture, intricate woodwork, and serene atmosphere create a tranquil space for worship and contemplation. Visitors can also explore the temple's museum, showcasing artifacts that shed light on the history of Chinese immigrants in Melaka.

7. Kapitan Keling Mosque, Penang:

Named after the Indian Muslim leader, Kapitan Keling Mosque in Penang is a stunning example of Indo-Moorish architecture. Its towering minarets, intricate carvings, and vibrant tiles make it a visual delight. Visitors can join guided tours to learn about the mosque's history and witness the harmonious coexistence of different religious communities in Malaysia.

8. Arulmigu Sri Rajakaliamman Glass Temple, Johor:

This unique Hindu temple in Johor Bahru is entirely made of glass, adorned with intricate glass sculptures and colorful mosaics. The temple's modern design and sparkling interior create a mesmerizing ambiance. Devotees and visitors can marvel at the intricacy of the glasswork and witness the grandeur of Hindu rituals.

9. Wat Chayamangkalaram, Penang:

Home to one of the world's largest reclining Buddha statues, Wat Chayamangkalaram is a Thai Buddhist temple in Penang. The 33-meter long gold-plated statue is an awe-inspiring sight, attracting visitors from far and wide. The temple also houses numerous other Buddha statues and offers a serene environment for meditation and contemplation.

10. Christ Church, Melaka:

A prominent landmark in Melaka, Christ Church is a testament to the city's colonial past. Built by the Dutch in the 18th century, this red-brick church stands as a symbol of Melaka's Christian heritage. Visitors can admire the church's unique architecture, explore the surrounding Dutch Square, and immerse themselves in the historical charm of the city.

Conclusion:

Malaysia's religious sites offer a glimpse into the country's diverse cultural heritage. Whether you are seeking spiritual enlightenment or simply interested in exploring the historical and architectural wonders, these top 10 religious sites in Malaysia are sure to leave a lasting impression. Embrace the harmony and coexistence of various religions as you embark on a journey of discovery through Malaysia's religious tapestry.

Chapter 22: Outdoor Activities in Malaysia

Introduction:

Malaysia, a tropical paradise nestled in Southeast Asia, offers a plethora of outdoor activities for adventure enthusiasts and nature lovers alike. From pristine rainforests to stunning beaches, this chapter will guide you through the top ten outdoor activities that will leave you in awe of Malaysia's natural beauty.

1. Trekking in Taman Negara:

Embark on an unforgettable trekking adventure in Taman Negara, Malaysia's oldest national park. With its dense rainforests, rugged terrains, and diverse wildlife, Taman Negara offers an unparalleled experience. Traverse the Canopy Walkway, spot exotic animals, and immerse yourself in the rich biodiversity of this enchanting rainforest.

2. Scuba Diving in Sipadan:

Dive into the crystal-clear waters surrounding Sipadan Island, renowned as one of the world's best diving destinations. Marvel at the vibrant coral reefs teeming with marine life, including turtles, sharks, and rays. Sipadan's underwater world guarantees an awe-inspiring experience for both beginners and seasoned divers.

3. White Water Rafting in Sungai Kampar:

Seek an adrenaline rush as you navigate the rapids of Sungai Kampar, located in Perak. With its thrilling twists and turns, this river offers an exhilarating white water rafting experience. Enjoy the lush greenery and cascading waterfalls as you conquer the rapids, making it a perfect activity for adventure seekers.

4. Paragliding in Kundasang:

Soar through the skies and witness the breathtaking landscapes of Kundasang, Sabah, while paragliding. Feel the wind beneath your wings as you glide above the majestic Mount Kinabalu and the picturesque valleys below. This exhilarating activity provides a unique perspective of Malaysia's natural wonders.

5. Jungle Safari in Borneo:

Embark on a once-in-a-lifetime jungle safari in Borneo, home to some of the world's most diverse ecosystems. Explore the lush rainforests and encounter rare wildlife, such as orangutans, proboscis monkeys, and pygmy elephants. Immerse yourself in the wonders of nature as you trek through the dense foliage and witness the beauty of Borneo's wildlife up close.

6. Rock Climbing in Batu Caves:

Challenge yourself with a thrilling rock climbing adventure at Batu Caves, just outside Kuala Lumpur. Scale the limestone cliffs and enjoy panoramic views of the city skyline. Whether you're a beginner or an experienced climber, Batu Caves offers a variety of routes suitable for all skill levels.

7. Island Hopping in Langkawi:

Explore the stunning archipelago of Langkawi by embarking on an island-hopping tour. Hop from one idyllic island to another, basking in the sun on pristine beaches, snorkeling in turquoise waters, and discovering hidden caves. Langkawi's natural beauty is sure to leave you mesmerized.

8. Canyoning in Ulu Slim:

Experience the thrill of canyoning in Ulu Slim, Perak, where you'll navigate through gushing waterfalls, natural slides, and rocky pools. This adrenaline-pumping activity combines hiking, swimming, and abseiling, providing an unforgettable adventure amidst Malaysia's lush landscapes.

9. Cycling in Cameron Highlands:

Embark on a cycling adventure through the scenic landscapes of Cameron Highlands. Pedal through tea plantations, strawberry farms, and rolling hills, immersing yourself in the cool climate and breathtaking vistas. Cycling enthusiasts will find this activity both invigorating and rewarding.

10. Bird Watching in Fraser's Hill:

Discover the avian wonders of Fraser's Hill, a haven for bird enthusiasts. With over 250 species of birds, including the rare Malaysian pheasant and hornbills, this hill station offers an ideal setting for bird watching. Explore the lush forests, listen to the melodic calls, and witness the vibrant plumage of Malaysia's feathered residents.

Conclusion:

Malaysia's outdoor activities promise an unforgettable experience for adventure seekers and nature lovers. From trekking through ancient rainforests to diving into vibrant underwater worlds, Malaysia's natural wonders will leave you in awe. So, pack your bags, embrace the spirit of adventure, and embark on a journey to discover the breathtaking outdoor beauty that Malaysia has to offer.

Chapter 23: Shopping in Malaysia

Introduction:

Malaysia is renowned for its vibrant shopping scene, offering a plethora of options for all kinds of shoppers. From bustling markets to luxurious malls, this chapter will guide you through the best places to shop in Malaysia and provide insights on what to buy, ensuring an unforgettable shopping experience.

1. Kuala Lumpur: The Shopper's Paradise

Kuala Lumpur, the capital city of Malaysia, is a shopaholic's dream come true. The city boasts an array of shopping destinations, catering to all budgets and tastes. From high-end fashion brands in Suria KLCC to affordable street shopping in Petaling Street, Kuala Lumpur has it all. Don't miss out on exploring the Central Market, where you can find traditional handicrafts, batik prints, and unique souvenirs.

2. Penang: A Melting Pot of Cultures and Shopping

Penang, known for its rich heritage and delicious street food, is also a fantastic place to indulge in some retail therapy. Georgetown, the capital city of Penang, is home to numerous boutique stores, art galleries, and antique shops. Armenian Street and Muntri Street are popular spots to find unique artworks, handcrafted jewelry, and vintage items. Additionally, don't forget to visit the Batu Ferringhi Night Market for great bargains on clothing, accessories, and local handicrafts.

3. Johor Bahru: Affordable Shopping Haven

Located at the southern tip of Malaysia, Johor Bahru offers an excellent opportunity for budget shoppers. The city is known for its numerous shopping malls, such as Johor Bahru City Square and KSL City Mall, where you can find a wide variety of products at affordable prices. For a unique shopping experience, head to Jalan Tan Hiok Nee, a street filled with charming cafes, boutique stores, and traditional Chinese medicine shops.

4. Langkawi: A Duty-Free Shopper's Paradise

Langkawi, a beautiful island in Malaysia, is not only known for its stunning beaches but also for being a duty-free shopping destination. The main shopping areas in Langkawi are Kuah Town and Pantai Cenang, where you can find a wide range of duty-free products, including alcohol, chocolates, cosmetics, and electronics. Take advantage of the tax-free prices and indulge in some guilt-free shopping.

5. Sabah: Treasures from the Borneo Rainforest

If you're looking for unique souvenirs and traditional handicrafts, Sabah is the place to be. Visit the Kota Kinabalu Handicraft Market, where you can find a wide variety of local products such as woven baskets, wood carvings, and traditional textiles. Don't forget to explore Gaya Street Sunday Market, a vibrant market offering an array of local delicacies, fresh produce, and handicrafts.

Conclusion:

Shopping in Malaysia is an adventure in itself, offering a wide range of shopping experiences across the country. Whether you're looking for luxury brands, affordable bargains, or traditional handicrafts, Malaysia has it all. So, grab your shopping bags and get ready to explore the diverse and exciting shopping scene this beautiful country has to offer.

Chapter 24: Nightlife in Malaysia

Introduction:

When the sun sets in Malaysia, a vibrant and exciting nightlife scene comes to life. From bustling cities to idyllic beachside towns, Malaysia offers a diverse range of options for those seeking an unforgettable night out. In this chapter, we will explore some of the best places to go out at night in Malaysia and provide you with valuable tips for enjoying the country's vibrant nightlife.

1. Kuala Lumpur: The City that Never Sleeps

Kuala Lumpur, the capital city of Malaysia, is known for its lively and energetic nightlife. The city offers a plethora of options to suit every taste and preference. Start your evening by exploring the famous Changkat Bukit Bintang, a street lined with vibrant bars and clubs. Here, you can enjoy live music, dance the night away, and indulge in delicious cocktails. For a more upscale experience, head to the rooftop bars in the city center, such as SkyBar or Marini's on 57, where you can enjoy breathtaking views of the city skyline while sipping on your favorite drink.

2. Penang: A Fusion of Culture and Entertainment

Penang, a UNESCO World Heritage Site, is not only famous for its historical charm but also for its lively nightlife. Georgetown, the capital city of Penang, offers a vibrant street art scene that comes to life at night. Explore the narrow streets of Armenian Street and Love Lane, where you will find charming bars and pubs hidden within colonial-era buildings. For a unique experience, visit the Hin Bus Depot, an art space that transforms into a trendy night market on weekends, offering a mix of local food, live music, and art exhibitions.

3. Langkawi: Beachside Fun and Entertainment

Langkawi, an archipelago of 99 islands, is known for its stunning beaches and natural beauty. When the sun sets, the island transforms into a hub of beachside bars and clubs. Pantai Cenang, the most popular beach in Langkawi, is lined with lively bars and restaurants where you can enjoy live music, fire shows, and beachside parties. For a more relaxed atmosphere, head to Pantai Tengah, where you can unwind with a cocktail while listening to the sound of the waves crashing against the shore.

4. Kota Kinabalu: A Taste of Borneo's Nightlife

Kota Kinabalu, the capital city of Sabah, offers a unique blend of modern entertainment and traditional culture. Start your evening at the waterfront area, where you can enjoy a scenic sunset while sipping on a refreshing drink. As the night progresses, head to the Filipino Market, a bustling night market where you can sample local delicacies, shop for souvenirs, and enjoy live performances by local musicians. For a more vibrant experience, visit the clubs and bars along Jalan Tun Fuad Stephens, where you can dance to a mix of local and international music.

Tips for Enjoying the Nightlife in Malaysia:

1. Dress Code: While Malaysia is a relatively conservative country, the dress code for nightlife is generally more relaxed. However, it is advisable to dress appropriately and avoid wearing revealing or offensive clothing, especially in more traditional areas.

2. Safety: As with any nightlife scene, it is important to prioritize your safety. Stick to well-lit and crowded areas, avoid walking alone at night, and be cautious of your belongings.

3. Transportation: Plan your transportation in advance, especially if you plan on visiting multiple venues in one night. Utilize ride-hailing services or book a taxi to ensure a safe journey back to your accommodation.

4. Local Etiquette: Respect the local culture and customs while enjoying the nightlife in Malaysia. Avoid excessive public displays of affection and be mindful of local sensitivities.

Conclusion:

Malaysia's nightlife scene offers a diverse range of experiences, from the vibrant city lights of Kuala Lumpur to the idyllic beachside bars of Langkawi. By following the tips provided in this chapter, you can enjoy a memorable and safe night out in Malaysia. So, get ready to immerse yourself in the electrifying energy of Malaysia's nightlife and create unforgettable memories.

Chapter 25: Festivals and Events in Malaysia

Introduction:

Malaysia is a culturally diverse nation that celebrates a multitude of festivals and events throughout the year. From religious observances to cultural extravaganzas, these festivities showcase the vibrant spirit and rich heritage of the Malaysian people. In this chapter, we will explore some of the major festivals and events that take place in Malaysia, offering you a glimpse into the country's colorful tapestry of traditions and celebrations.

1. Hari Raya Aidilfitri:

Hari Raya Aidilfitri, also known as Eid al-Fitr, is one of the most important festivals celebrated by Muslims in Malaysia. It marks the end of Ramadan, the holy month of fasting. During this joyous occasion, families and friends come together to seek forgiveness, exchange gifts, and indulge in delicious traditional Malay cuisine. The streets come alive with vibrant decorations, and it is customary to visit open houses to extend warm greetings and share festive treats.

2. Thaipusam:

Thaipusam is a Hindu festival celebrated by the Tamil community in Malaysia. Devotees embark on a pilgrimage to Batu Caves, a famous limestone hill temple near Kuala Lumpur. They carry ornately decorated kavadis (burdens) attached to their bodies through piercings and walk barefoot up the steep steps of the caves. The atmosphere is electrifying, with devotees chanting prayers and performing various acts of devotion, creating a truly awe-inspiring spectacle.

3. Chinese New Year:

Chinese New Year, also known as the Spring Festival, is a grand celebration for the Chinese community in Malaysia. It is a time for family reunions, feasting, and honoring ancestors. The streets are adorned with red lanterns, and lion and dragon dances fill the air with excitement and energy. Temples and homes are decorated with auspicious symbols, and the exchange of mandarin oranges signifies good luck and prosperity for the coming year.

4. Rainforest World Music Festival:

The Rainforest World Music Festival is an annual three-day music festival held in Sarawak, East Malaysia. It brings together renowned musicians from around the world to showcase their traditional music and cultural heritage. The festival promotes cross-cultural understanding and appreciation for indigenous music, offering visitors a unique opportunity to immerse themselves in the rhythms and melodies of different cultures against the backdrop of the lush Borneo rainforest.

5. George Town Festival:

George Town Festival is a month-long celebration of arts, culture, and heritage held in Penang. It features a diverse range of performances, exhibitions, workshops, and installations by local and international artists. The festival aims to showcase Penang's artistic and creative talent while preserving its unique heritage. Visitors can experience a fusion of traditional and contemporary art forms, including music, dance, theater, and visual arts, all set amidst the charming streets of George Town.

Conclusion:

Malaysia's festivals and events offer a kaleidoscope of colors, flavors, and traditions that reflect the country's multicultural tapestry. Whether you're seeking spiritual enlightenment, cultural immersion, or simply a joyous celebration, Malaysia's calendar is filled with opportunities to experience the warmth and hospitality of its people. As you explore the festivals and events mentioned in this chapter, you will gain a deeper understanding of Malaysia's rich cultural heritage and create lasting memories of your visit to this enchanting nation.

Chapter 26: Activities for Couples in Malaysia

Introduction:

Malaysia, with its stunning landscapes, vibrant culture, and warm hospitality, offers an array of romantic activities for couples. Whether you are seeking adventure or relaxation, this chapter will guide you through the top 10 most romantic activities for couples in Malaysia.

1. Sunset Cruise in Langkawi:

Embark on a romantic sunset cruise in Langkawi, where you and your partner can sail along the stunning coastline while being mesmerized by the breathtaking sunset. Enjoy a glass of champagne, indulge in a delicious dinner, and create unforgettable memories together.

2. Jungle Trekking in Taman Negara:

For adventure-seeking couples, a jungle trekking experience in Taman Negara is a must. Hold hands as you navigate through lush rainforests, encounter exotic wildlife, and witness the beauty of Malaysia's oldest national park.

3. Hot Air Balloon Ride in Putrajaya:

Take your love to new heights with a hot air balloon ride in Putrajaya. Soar above the city's skyline and marvel at the picturesque landscapes below. This serene and romantic experience will leave you with memories to cherish forever.

4. Island Hopping in Perhentian Islands:

Escape to the tropical paradise of the Perhentian Islands, where you can embark on an island-hopping adventure. Explore crystal-clear waters, snorkel alongside vibrant marine life, and relax on pristine white sandy beaches with your loved one.

5. Spa Retreat in Cameron Highlands:

Indulge in a romantic spa retreat amidst the cool climate of Cameron Highlands. Pamper yourselves with rejuvenating massages, enjoy aromatic tea baths, and unwind in the tranquil ambiance of the highlands.

6. River Safari in Kinabatangan:

Immerse yourselves in the wonders of nature with a river safari in Kinabatangan. Cruise along the river, spot proboscis monkeys swinging from trees, witness vibrant bird species, and embrace the serenity of the Borneo rainforest.

7. Cultural Experience in Georgetown, Penang:

Discover the rich cultural heritage of Malaysia by exploring the streets of Georgetown in Penang. Wander through historic sites, admire colorful street art, savor delicious street food, and immerse yourselves in the vibrant atmosphere of this UNESCO World Heritage Site.

8. Helicopter Ride over Kuala Lumpur:

For a truly unforgettable experience, take a helicopter ride over the iconic cityscape of Kuala Lumpur. Admire the Petronas Twin Towers, the bustling city below, and the panoramic views that stretch as far as the eye can see.

9. Romantic Dinner in the Sky, Kuala Lumpur:

Elevate your dining experience by indulging in a romantic dinner in the sky. Suspended 50 meters above the ground, enjoy a gourmet meal while overlooking the dazzling skyline of Kuala Lumpur, creating a truly magical evening.

10. Beach Picnic in the Perhentian Islands:

Escape to a secluded beach in the Perhentian Islands and enjoy a romantic picnic with your loved one. Surrounded by turquoise waters and pristine white sand, relish in each other's company while savoring a delicious meal amidst the breathtaking scenery.

Conclusion:

From enchanting sunsets to thrilling adventures, Malaysia offers a myriad of romantic activities for couples. Whether you prefer relaxation or excitement, these top 10 activities will undoubtedly create unforgettable memories and strengthen the bond between you and your partner.

Chapter 27: Activities for Solo Travelers in Malaysia

Introduction:

Malaysia, a vibrant and diverse country in Southeast Asia, offers a plethora of exciting activities for solo travelers. From exploring breathtaking natural landscapes to immersing oneself in rich cultural experiences, Malaysia has something for everyone. In this chapter, we will highlight the top 10 activities that are perfect for solo travelers seeking adventure, relaxation, and self-discovery.

1. Trekking in Taman Negara:

Embark on an unforgettable solo trekking adventure in Taman Negara, one of the world's oldest rainforests. Hike through dense jungles, cross hanging bridges, and spot exotic wildlife. With guided tours available, you can explore this natural wonder at your own pace while feeling the thrill of being in the heart of the wilderness.

2. Scuba Diving in Sipadan:

For solo travelers seeking underwater adventures, Sipadan Island is a must-visit destination. Dive into the crystal-clear waters of the Celebes Sea and discover an abundance of marine life, including turtles, sharks, and colorful coral reefs. With several dive operators offering solo-friendly packages, you can explore the depths of the ocean in a safe and enjoyable manner.

3. Food Exploration in Penang:

Known as the food capital of Malaysia, Penang is a haven for solo travelers who love to indulge in culinary delights. Wander through the bustling streets of George Town and savor the diverse flavors of Malaysian cuisine. From street food stalls to trendy cafes, Penang offers a gastronomic adventure that will tantalize your taste buds.

4. Yoga Retreat in Langkawi:

Escape the hustle and bustle of everyday life by joining a yoga retreat in the serene island of Langkawi. Solo travelers can rejuvenate their mind, body, and soul amidst breathtaking landscapes. With experienced instructors guiding you through yoga sessions, meditation, and wellness activities, this retreat provides a perfect opportunity for self-reflection and relaxation.

5. Cultural Immersion in Melaka:

Immerse yourself in the rich cultural heritage of Malaysia by visiting the historical city of Melaka. Solo travelers can explore the UNESCO World Heritage sites, wander through vibrant streets adorned with colorful murals, and indulge in the local cuisine. Don't miss the chance to experience the unique Baba-Nyonya culture, which is a fusion of Chinese and Malay traditions.

6. Wildlife Safari in Borneo:

Embark on a wildlife safari in Borneo, home to some of the world's most diverse ecosystems. Solo travelers can witness orangutans swinging through the trees, encounter proboscis monkeys, and explore lush rainforests. With ethical tour operators offering solo-friendly packages, you can contribute to conservation efforts while enjoying an unforgettable wildlife experience.

7. Island Hopping in Perhentian Islands:

Escape to the pristine beaches of the Perhentian Islands, where solo travelers can indulge in a tropical paradise. Hop from one breathtaking island to another, snorkel in crystal-clear waters, and soak up the sun on white sandy beaches. With budget-friendly accommodations and a laid-back atmosphere, these islands are perfect for solo relaxation and beach exploration.

8. Heritage Walk in Kuala Lumpur:

Discover the vibrant city of Kuala Lumpur through a heritage walk that takes you through its colonial past and modern developments. Solo travelers can explore iconic landmarks such as the Petronas Twin Towers, Merdeka Square, and the vibrant Chinatown. With a mix of architectural wonders, delicious street food, and bustling markets, Kuala Lumpur offers a dynamic solo adventure.

9. River Cruising in Sarawak:

Experience the tranquility of the Sarawak River by embarking on a river cruise. Solo travelers can witness the beauty of the mangrove forests, spot wildlife along the riverbanks, and immerse themselves in the local culture. With knowledgeable guides sharing stories about the region's history and biodiversity, this river cruise offers a unique perspective on Sarawak's natural wonders.

10. Cycling in Cameron Highlands:

For solo travelers who enjoy outdoor activities, cycling through the scenic landscapes of Cameron Highlands is a must-do. Pedal your way through tea plantations, strawberry farms, and lush valleys, while enjoying the cool climate of this hill station. With numerous cycling routes available, you can explore at your own pace and soak in the beauty of Malaysia's highlands.

Conclusion:

Malaysia provides solo travelers with a diverse range of activities that cater to various interests and preferences. From thrilling adventures to cultural immersions, this chapter has highlighted the top 10 activities that will make your solo journey in Malaysia truly unforgettable. Embrace the freedom of solo travel and embark on a memorable exploration of this enchanting country.

Chapter 28: Budget-friendly activities in Malaysia

Introduction:

Malaysia is a vibrant and diverse country that offers a wide range of attractions for travelers on a budget. From stunning natural landscapes to cultural experiences, there are plenty of affordable activities to enjoy without breaking the bank. In this chapter, we will explore the top 10 budget-friendly activities in Malaysia, ensuring that you can make the most of your visit while keeping your wallet happy.

1. Explore the Petronas Twin Towers:

The iconic Petronas Twin Towers in Kuala Lumpur are a must-visit attraction, and luckily, you can enjoy the experience without spending a fortune. While tickets to the observation deck can be pricey, you can still marvel at the towers from the outside and take stunning photos for free. Visit during the evening to witness the towers beautifully illuminated against the night sky.

2. Wander through the Batu Caves:

Located just outside Kuala Lumpur, the Batu Caves are a series of limestone caves that house Hindu temples and shrines. Entrance to the caves is free, allowing you to explore the intricate cave formations and witness religious ceremonies. Remember to dress modestly and be prepared to climb the 272 steps leading to the main cave.

3. Immerse yourself in street art in Penang:

Penang is renowned for its vibrant street art scene, with murals adorning the walls of George Town. Take a leisurely stroll through the city, spotting these captivating artworks and capturing Instagram-worthy pictures. This activity is not only budget-friendly but also a great way to explore the rich cultural heritage of Penang.

4. Relax on Langkawi's stunning beaches:

Langkawi, a popular island destination, offers pristine beaches with crystal-clear waters and soft white sand. Spend a day lounging on the beach, swimming, and enjoying the breathtaking views. Pack a picnic and make the most of the free public facilities available, ensuring a memorable and budget-friendly day.

5. Trek through the rainforests of Taman Negara:

For nature enthusiasts, Taman Negara National Park is a must-visit destination. Embark on a budget-friendly trek through the oldest rainforest in the world, marveling at the diverse flora and fauna along the way. Don't forget to visit the Canopy Walkway, offering a unique perspective of the rainforest from above.

6. Discover the historical sites of Melaka:

Melaka is a UNESCO World Heritage Site known for its rich history and cultural significance. Explore the city's historical sites, such as St. Paul's Church, A Famosa Fort, and Jonker Street. Immerse yourself in the vibrant atmosphere, sample local street food, and browse through the bustling night market, all without spending a fortune.

7. Visit the Perhentian Islands:

Escape the hustle and bustle of city life and head to the budget-friendly Perhentian Islands. These tropical paradises offer stunning beaches, crystal-clear waters, and abundant marine life. Snorkel or dive in the coral reefs, go hiking, or simply relax on the beach, all while enjoying the beauty of nature.

8. Explore the Cameron Highlands:

The Cameron Highlands provide a refreshing escape from Malaysia's tropical climate. Embark on scenic hikes through tea plantations, visit strawberry farms, and enjoy the cool climate. The highlands offer numerous affordable accommodations, making it an ideal destination for budget-conscious travelers.

9. Experience local markets:

One of the best ways to immerse yourself in the local culture is by visiting the vibrant markets in Malaysia. Explore the Central Market in Kuala Lumpur, the Night Market in Kota Kinabalu, or the Pasar Malam in various towns. Here, you can sample local delicacies, shop for souvenirs, and experience the lively atmosphere, all at affordable prices.

10. Enjoy street food delights:

No visit to Malaysia is complete without indulging in its world-renowned street food. From mouthwatering satay to delicious nasi lemak, the variety of flavors will leave you wanting more. Seek out local food stalls and hawker centers, which offer affordable and authentic culinary experiences, allowing you to savor Malaysia's gastronomic delights without breaking the bank.

Conclusion:

Malaysia offers an array of budget-friendly activities that cater to all types of travelers. From cultural experiences to natural wonders, this chapter has highlighted the top 10 affordable activities that will allow you to make the most of your visit while staying within your budget. Embrace the diversity, immerse yourself in the local culture, and create unforgettable memories without compromising your wallet.

Chapter 29: Off-the-beaten-path Activities in Malaysia

Introduction:

Malaysia is renowned for its stunning natural landscapes, vibrant cultural diversity, and bustling cities. While popular tourist attractions like the Petronas Twin Towers and Langkawi Island are undoubtedly worth a visit, there is a wealth of off-the-beaten-path activities that offer a unique and authentic Malaysian experience. In this chapter, we will explore the top 10 off-the-beaten-path activities that will take you on a journey of discovery through the hidden gems of Malaysia.

1. Exploring the Bornean Rainforest:

Venture deep into the heart of Borneo, where a vast expanse of untouched rainforest awaits. Embark on a guided trek to discover rare wildlife such as orangutans, pygmy elephants, and proboscis monkeys. Immerse yourself in the rich biodiversity and learn about the conservation efforts that aim to protect this fragile ecosystem.

2. Discovering the Hidden Temples of Penang:

Beyond the bustling streets of George Town lies a treasure trove of hidden temples. Take a leisurely stroll through the narrow lanes and uncover ornate Chinese, Hindu, and Thai temples. Marvel at the intricate architecture, vibrant colors, and spiritual ambiance that these lesser-known temples offer.

3. Trekking the Mossy Forest of Cameron Highlands:

Escape the heat and venture into the enchanting Mossy Forest of Cameron Highlands. Explore the mist-covered trails, surrounded by ancient trees draped in moss and ferns. Discover unique flora and fauna, including the carnivorous pitcher plants and vibrant orchids that thrive in this cool and mystical environment.

4. Exploring the Underground Wonders of Mulu Caves:

Embark on an unforgettable adventure in Mulu National Park, home to some of the world's most impressive cave systems. Traverse through the vast chambers of Deer Cave, marvel at the towering stalagmites and stalactites of Clearwater Cave, and witness the mesmerizing spectacle of millions of bats emerging from the caves at sunset.

5. Experiencing Traditional Village Life in Sarawak:

Step back in time and immerse yourself in the rich cultural heritage of Sarawak's traditional villages. Stay in a longhouse, a communal dwelling that offers a glimpse into the daily lives of the indigenous tribes. Engage in traditional activities, such as blowpipe shooting, weaving, and participating in age-old rituals.

6. Snorkeling in the Pristine Waters of Perhentian Islands:

Escape the crowds and discover the untouched beauty of the Perhentian Islands. Dive into crystal-clear waters teeming with vibrant coral reefs and colorful marine life. Snorkel alongside sea turtles, explore hidden coves, and relax on secluded beaches, far away from the tourist hotspots.

7. Cycling through Rural Landscapes of Sekinchan:

Embark on a cycling adventure through the picturesque landscapes of Sekinchan. Pedal past lush paddy fields, quaint fishing villages, and traditional Chinese temples. Immerse yourself in the rural charm, witness the local way of life, and savor freshly harvested seafood and local delicacies.

8. River Safari in Kinabatangan:

Embark on a river safari along the Kinabatangan River, one of the best places in Malaysia to spot wildlife. Cruise through mangrove forests and oxbow lakes, keeping an eye out for proboscis monkeys, Bornean pygmy elephants, and a myriad of bird species. Experience the tranquility of this pristine wilderness.

9. Exploring the Street Art of Ipoh:

Uncover the vibrant street art scene of Ipoh, a city known for its colonial charm and delicious food. Wander through the old town's narrow alleys and be captivated by the colorful murals that adorn the walls. Discover hidden art pieces, each with its own story to tell, and get a taste of the local art scene.

10. Hiking to the Hidden Waterfalls of Taman Negara:

Embark on a hiking expedition through Taman Negara, Malaysia's oldest national park. Trek through dense rainforest, cross suspension bridges, and discover hidden waterfalls cascading into crystal-clear pools. Take a refreshing dip, surrounded by the sights and sounds of nature, and create memories that will last a lifetime.

Conclusion:

Malaysia offers a multitude of off-the-beaten-path activities that will reward you with unforgettable experiences and a deeper understanding of the country's diverse culture and natural wonders. From exploring hidden temples to trekking through ancient rainforests, each activity promises an authentic Malaysian adventure. Step away from the well-trodden path and embark on a journey of discovery, where the true essence of Malaysia awaits.

Chapter 30: Sustainable Tourism Experiences in Malaysia

Introduction:

Malaysia, a vibrant and diverse country located in Southeast Asia, is known for its breathtaking landscapes, rich cultural heritage, and warm hospitality. In recent years, Malaysia has also emerged as a leader in sustainable tourism, offering travelers unique experiences that not only showcase the country's natural beauty but also promote environmental conservation and support local communities. In this chapter, we will explore the top 10 sustainable tourism experiences in Malaysia, providing you with an unforgettable journey that respects and preserves the country's natural and cultural treasures.

1. Exploring the Rainforests of Borneo:

Embark on a once-in-a-lifetime adventure to Borneo, home to one of the oldest rainforests in the world. Join a sustainable eco-tourism program that allows you to explore the lush jungles while supporting local conservation efforts and indigenous communities.

2. Turtle Conservation in Terengganu:

Visit the pristine beaches of Terengganu and participate in a turtle conservation program. Witness the incredible sight of turtles nesting and hatching while learning about the importance of protecting these endangered species and their habitats.

3. Sustainable Farming in Cameron Highlands:

Immerse yourself in the cool highlands of Cameron and discover sustainable farming practices. Engage in organic farming activities, learn about agro-tourism, and indulge in farm-to-table experiences, supporting local farmers and reducing your carbon footprint.

4. Homestay Experiences in Kampung Morten:

Experience the warmth of Malaysian hospitality by staying with a local family in Kampung Morten, a traditional Malay village. Engage in cultural exchanges, participate in traditional activities, and contribute directly to the local community's economy.

5. River Safari in Kinabatangan:

Embark on a river safari along the Kinabatangan River, where you can spot a wide variety of wildlife, including orangutans, proboscis monkeys, and pygmy elephants. Choose a tour operator committed to sustainable practices and wildlife conservation.

6. Sustainable Island Hopping in Langkawi:

Discover the stunning islands of Langkawi while supporting sustainable tourism initiatives. Choose eco-friendly tour operators that prioritize marine conservation, responsible snorkeling, and protection of fragile ecosystems.

7. Cultural Conservation in George Town:

Explore the UNESCO World Heritage Site of George Town, Penang, and contribute to the preservation of its unique cultural heritage. Engage in heritage walks, visit traditional trades, and support local artisans and craftsmen.

8. Eco-friendly Diving in Sipadan:

Dive into the crystal-clear waters of Sipadan Island, a world-renowned diving destination. Choose dive operators that follow sustainable diving practices, protecting the fragile coral reefs and marine life.

9. Sustainable Trekking in Taman Negara:

Embark on a trekking adventure in Taman Negara, one of the oldest rainforests in the world. Opt for responsible tour operators that prioritize conservation, educate visitors on the importance of preserving the ecosystem, and support local communities.

10. Wildlife Conservation in Sepilok:

Visit the Sepilok Orangutan Rehabilitation Centre and witness the incredible work being done to protect and rehabilitate orangutans. Learn about the conservation efforts and support the center's initiatives through responsible tourism practices.

Conclusion:

Malaysia offers a plethora of sustainable tourism experiences that allow travelers to connect with nature, immerse themselves in local cultures, and contribute to the preservation of the country's natural and cultural heritage. By choosing responsible tour operators, supporting local communities, and practicing sustainable travel behaviors, you can make a positive impact while creating unforgettable memories in this beautiful and diverse country.

Chapter 31: Responsible Tourism Experiences in Malaysia

Introduction:

Malaysia, a vibrant and diverse country in Southeast Asia, offers a plethora of responsible tourism experiences that allow travelers to explore its natural wonders, engage with local communities, and contribute to sustainable development. From conservation efforts to cultural immersion, this chapter will showcase the top 10 responsible tourism experiences in Malaysia, ensuring an unforgettable and ethical journey for every traveler.

1. Borneo Rainforest Conservation:

Embark on a journey to Borneo, home to one of the oldest rainforests in the world. Engage with local conservation organizations that focus on protecting endangered species, such as orangutans and pygmy elephants. Participate in volunteer programs or eco-tours that contribute directly to the preservation of this unique ecosystem.

2. Sustainable Island Hopping in Langkawi:

Explore the stunning archipelago of Langkawi while supporting sustainable practices. Choose eco-friendly boat operators that prioritize marine conservation, minimize pollution, and promote responsible snorkeling and diving activities. Discover the diverse marine life, pristine beaches, and hidden caves while leaving only footprints behind.

3. Community-Based Tourism in Kampung Stay:

Escape the bustling cities and immerse yourself in the charm of traditional Malaysian villages. Experience the warmth of local hospitality by staying in a homestay in Kampung Stay, where you can actively participate in the daily activities of the community. Learn about their customs, traditions, and crafts while supporting the local economy.

4. Responsible Wildlife Encounters in Sepilok:

Visit the renowned Sepilok Orangutan Rehabilitation Centre in Sabah, where orphaned orangutans are rehabilitated and released back into the wild. Observe these incredible creatures in their natural habitat while respecting their space and following ethical guidelines. By visiting, you contribute to the conservation efforts and awareness campaigns.

5. Sustainable Farming in Cameron Highlands:

Discover the lush landscapes of the Cameron Highlands and engage in sustainable farming practices. Join local farmers in their daily routines, learn about organic cultivation methods, and taste freshly harvested produce. By supporting these sustainable agricultural initiatives, you contribute to the preservation of the region's biodiversity.

6. Responsible Diving in Sipadan:

Dive into the crystal-clear waters of Sipadan Island, renowned for its vibrant coral reefs and diverse marine life. Choose responsible dive operators that prioritize reef conservation and follow sustainable diving practices. By adhering to responsible guidelines, you can protect the fragile ecosystem while enjoying an unforgettable underwater experience.

7. Turtle Conservation in Terengganu:

Witness the incredible nesting process of endangered sea turtles on the pristine beaches of Terengganu. Join local conservation organizations to learn about their efforts in protecting these magnificent creatures. Participate in turtle releases, beach clean-ups, and educational programs to contribute to their survival and raise awareness.

8. Cultural Preservation in George Town:

Explore the UNESCO World Heritage Site of George Town in Penang, where history and culture intertwine. Support local artisans, craftsmen, and traditional businesses that strive to preserve the city's unique heritage. Engage in cultural workshops, taste authentic local cuisine, and appreciate the architectural marvels that make George Town so special.

9. Sustainable Trekking in Taman Negara:

Embark on an eco-adventure in Taman Negara, Malaysia's oldest national park. Choose responsible trekking operators that prioritize environmental conservation and respect the park's biodiversity. Traverse through ancient rainforests, spot rare wildlife, and contribute to the park's sustainability by adhering to designated trails and guidelines.

10. Responsible Urban Exploration in Kuala Lumpur:

Discover the vibrant capital city of Kuala Lumpur while supporting responsible tourism practices. Choose accommodations that prioritize sustainability, engage in local community tours, and support ethical businesses. By being mindful of your environmental impact and respecting local customs, you can contribute to the city's sustainable development.

Conclusion:

Malaysia offers a wide array of responsible tourism experiences that allow travelers to explore the country's natural wonders, engage with local communities, and contribute to sustainable development. By choosing these top 10 experiences, you can ensure an ethical and truthful journey that leaves a positive impact on Malaysia's environment, wildlife, and cultural heritage. Embark on this responsible tourism adventure and create memories that will last a lifetime while making a difference.

Chapter 32: Volunteer Opportunities in Malaysia

Introduction:

Malaysia, known for its rich culture, diverse landscapes, and warm hospitality, offers countless opportunities for travelers seeking to make a positive impact through volunteer work. In this chapter, we will explore the top ten volunteer opportunities in Malaysia, providing you with unique and truthful insights to help you choose the perfect volunteering experience.

1. Wildlife Conservation:

Malaysia is home to a plethora of unique wildlife species, such as orangutans, tigers, and elephants. Volunteer programs focusing on wildlife conservation allow you to contribute to the preservation of these endangered species. Join hands with local organizations, assist in research projects, and help protect Malaysia's incredible biodiversity.

2. Marine Conservation:

With its stunning coral reefs and diverse marine life, Malaysia offers an ideal environment for those passionate about marine conservation. Engage in activities like coral reef restoration, turtle conservation, and marine research, while contributing to the sustainable development of Malaysia's marine ecosystems.

3. Orangutan Rehabilitation Centers:

Malaysia is renowned for its efforts in rehabilitating and protecting orangutans. Volunteer at one of the many orangutan rehabilitation centers, where you can assist in feeding, cleaning, and caring for these intelligent creatures. Contribute to their well-being and support their journey towards a better future.

4. Teaching English:

If you have a passion for teaching, consider volunteering at schools or community centers in rural areas of Malaysia. Help improve the

English language skills of local children, empowering them with better opportunities for the future. Experience the joy of making a lasting impact on their lives.

5. Community Development:

Various organizations in Malaysia focus on community development projects, aiming to uplift marginalized communities. Volunteer in programs that involve building homes, improving infrastructure, or providing healthcare and education facilities. Contribute to the betterment of local communities and witness the positive change firsthand.

6. Sustainable Farming:

Malaysia's fertile land and tropical climate provide excellent opportunities for sustainable farming practices. Join volunteer projects that promote organic farming, permaculture, or agroforestry. Learn about sustainable agricultural techniques while helping local farmers preserve their traditional practices.

7. Refugee Support:

Malaysia is home to a significant number of refugees seeking safety and a better life. Volunteer with organizations that provide support to refugees, offering services such as education, healthcare, and livelihood training. Make a difference in the lives of those who have been forced to flee their homelands.

8. Wildlife Rescue and Rehabilitation:

Volunteer with organizations dedicated to rescuing and rehabilitating injured or trafficked wildlife. Assist in the care and rehabilitation of animals, such as sun bears, pangolins, and hornbills. Contribute to the conservation efforts aimed at protecting Malaysia's unique wildlife.

9. Environmental Conservation:

Malaysia's breathtaking landscapes, including rainforests, mangroves, and national parks, require continuous conservation efforts. Participate in volunteer programs focused on environmental conservation, engaging in activities like reforestation, biodiversity monitoring, and eco-tourism initiatives.

10. Disaster Relief:

Malaysia is occasionally affected by natural disasters such as floods and landslides. Volunteer with disaster relief organizations to provide immediate assistance and support to affected communities. Contribute to relief efforts by providing aid, rehabilitation, and emotional support to those in need.

Conclusion:

Embarking on a volunteer journey in Malaysia allows you to experience the country in a unique and meaningful way. Whether you choose to work with wildlife, communities, or the environment, your efforts will contribute to the sustainable development and preservation of Malaysia's natural and cultural heritage. Embrace the opportunity to make a difference while creating unforgettable memories in this enchanting nation.

Chapter 33: Visas and Immigration Requirements for Malaysia

Introduction:

Welcome to Chapter 33 of our comprehensive tourist guide on Malaysia. In this chapter, we will provide you with a summary of the visa and immigration requirements for visiting this beautiful country. It is essential to familiarize yourself with these regulations to ensure a smooth and hassle-free entry into Malaysia.

1. Visa-Free Entry:

Malaysia offers visa-free entry to citizens of several countries for tourism purposes. Visitors from these countries can stay in Malaysia for a specified period without the need for a visa. The duration of stay varies depending on the nationality, ranging from 14 to 90 days. Some of the countries eligible for visa-free entry include the United States, United Kingdom, Canada, Australia, Japan, South Korea, and most European Union member states. It is important to check the official Malaysian immigration website or consult with the Malaysian Embassy or Consulate in your country to confirm your eligibility for visa-free entry.

2. Visa on Arrival:

For citizens of certain countries who are not eligible for visa-free entry, Malaysia offers a visa on arrival facility. This allows travelers to obtain a visa upon arrival at selected entry points in Malaysia. The visa on arrival is typically granted for a stay of up to 30 days and can be extended further if required. It is advisable to check the Malaysian immigration website or contact the Malaysian Embassy or Consulate in your country to confirm if you are eligible for a visa on arrival.

3. Tourist Visa:

If you are not eligible for visa-free entry or visa on arrival, you will need to apply for a tourist visa before your trip to Malaysia. The tourist visa allows visitors to stay in Malaysia for up to 90 days for tourism purposes. To obtain a tourist visa, you must submit an application to the nearest Malaysian Embassy or Consulate in your country. The application requirements may vary, but generally include a completed visa application form, a valid passport with a minimum of six months validity, passport-sized photographs, proof of accommodation and travel itinerary, proof of sufficient funds, and a return or onward ticket.

4. Multiple Entry Visa:

For frequent travelers to Malaysia, the Multiple Entry Visa (MEV) is a convenient option. The MEV allows multiple entries into Malaysia within a specified period, usually up to one year. Each entry allows a stay of up to 30 or 90 days, depending on the visa type. The MEV is suitable for individuals who frequently travel to Malaysia for business, social, or leisure purposes. To obtain an MEV, you must apply through the nearest Malaysian Embassy or Consulate in your country and fulfill the specific requirements, including proof of purpose of visit and financial capability.

Conclusion:

Understanding the visa and immigration requirements for Malaysia is crucial to ensure a smooth entry into the country. Whether you are eligible for visa-free entry, visa on arrival, or need to apply for a tourist visa or multiple entry visa, it is essential to follow the guidelines provided by the Malaysian authorities. Always check the official Malaysian immigration website or consult with the Malaysian Embassy or Consulate in your country for the most up-to-date and accurate information regarding visas and immigration requirements.

Chapter 34: Money and Banking in Malaysia

Introduction:

Welcome to the vibrant and diverse country of Malaysia! As you embark on your journey, it is essential to familiarize yourself with the local currency, exchange rates, ATMs, and credit card usage. This chapter aims to provide you with accurate and up-to-date information on money and banking in Malaysia, ensuring a smooth and hassle-free financial experience during your visit.

1. The Malaysian Currency:

The official currency of Malaysia is the Malaysian Ringgit (MYR). The currency is denoted by the symbol RM and is divided into 100 sen. Banknotes come in denominations of RM1, RM5, RM10, RM20, RM50, and RM100, while coins are available in denominations of 5 sen, 10 sen, 20 sen, and 50 sen. It is advisable to carry small denominations for convenience, especially when dealing with public transportation or small vendors.

2. Exchange Rates:

Exchange rates fluctuate daily, and it is crucial to stay updated with the latest rates. Major airports, banks, and money changers provide currency exchange services throughout Malaysia. It is advisable to compare rates and fees before making any exchanges to ensure you receive the best value for your money. Avoid exchanging currency at hotels, as they often offer less favorable rates.

3. ATMs and Cash Withdrawals:

ATMs are widely available in Malaysia, and most accept international debit and credit cards. Look for ATMs affiliated with major networks such as Visa, Mastercard, or Cirrus. While withdrawing cash, be cautious of your surroundings and use ATMs located in well-lit and secure areas. Inform your bank of your travel plans beforehand to prevent any card blocks due to suspicious activity.

4. Credit Card Usage:

Credit cards are widely accepted in Malaysia, especially in urban areas, high-end establishments, and tourist destinations. Visa and Mastercard are the most commonly accepted cards, followed by American Express and Diners Club. However, it is always advisable to carry some cash, as smaller establishments and local markets may prefer cash transactions or have limited card acceptance.

5. Precautions and Safety:

While Malaysia is generally safe, it is essential to take precautions to protect your finances. Avoid displaying large sums of cash in public, and be cautious of pickpockets in crowded areas. Keep your credit cards secure and always check your surroundings when using ATMs. It is also advisable to notify your bank of your travel plans to prevent any unexpected card blocks.

Conclusion:

Understanding the Malaysian currency, exchange rates, ATMs, and credit card usage will ensure a hassle-free financial experience during your visit. Remember to compare exchange rates, withdraw cash from secure locations, and carry small denominations for convenience. By following these guidelines, you can focus on exploring the rich culture, breathtaking landscapes, and warm hospitality that Malaysia has to offer. Safe travels and enjoy your time in this remarkable country!

Chapter 35: Communication in Malaysia

Introduction:

Communication plays a vital role in our daily lives, especially when we are traveling. In Malaysia, a diverse and vibrant country, staying connected with loved ones, accessing the internet, and sending mail is made easy and convenient. This chapter will provide a comprehensive overview of the phone system, internet access, and postal service in Malaysia, ensuring that visitors have a seamless communication experience throughout their stay.

1. The Phone System:

The phone system in Malaysia is highly reliable and efficient. The country is well-connected through a vast network of landlines and mobile phone coverage, ensuring that visitors can easily make both local and international calls. To make a local call within Malaysia, simply dial the desired phone number, including the area code. For international calls, dial the country code followed by the phone number. It is worth noting that prepaid SIM cards are widely available, allowing tourists to enjoy affordable rates and stay connected throughout their journey.

2. Internet Access:

In this digital age, reliable internet access is essential for travelers. Malaysia recognizes this need and offers a range of options to suit various requirements. Most hotels, cafes, and restaurants provide free Wi-Fi access, enabling visitors to stay connected while enjoying their meals or exploring the city. Additionally, numerous internet cafes are scattered throughout major cities, offering high-speed internet access for a nominal fee. For those who prefer to have internet access on the go, mobile data plans are available from local service providers, allowing tourists to stay connected wherever they may be.

3. Postal Service:

Sending mail and packages is a convenient and efficient process in Malaysia. The country boasts an extensive network of post offices, ensuring that visitors can easily access postal services. Post offices are typically open from Monday to Friday, with some branches operating on weekends as well. International mail and packages can be sent through various postal services, including Pos Malaysia, which offers reliable and affordable options. It is important to note that customs regulations should be adhered to when sending or receiving international mail, ensuring a smooth and hassle-free process.

Conclusion:

Communication in Malaysia is seamless and convenient, allowing visitors to stay connected with their loved ones and access the internet effortlessly. The phone system provides reliable coverage, ensuring that both local and international calls can be made without any hassle. Internet access is readily available, with free Wi-Fi hotspots, internet cafes, and mobile data plans catering to different needs. The postal service is efficient, making it easy to send and receive mail and packages. With these communication facilities in place, tourists can explore Malaysia with peace of mind, knowing that they can effortlessly stay connected throughout their journey.

Chapter 36: Health and Safety in Malaysia

Introduction:

As a responsible traveler, ensuring your health and safety should be a top priority. Malaysia, with its vibrant culture and stunning landscapes, offers a delightful experience for tourists. However, it is essential to be aware of the common health risks and safety tips to make your visit to Malaysia a safe and enjoyable one.

1. Vaccinations and Medical Precautions:

Before traveling to Malaysia, it is advisable to consult your healthcare provider or a travel clinic to ensure you are up to date on routine vaccinations. Additionally, certain vaccines such as Hepatitis A, Typhoid, and Japanese Encephalitis may be recommended based on the areas you plan to visit. Malaria prophylaxis may be required if you are traveling to rural or forested areas.

2. Food and Water Safety:

Malaysia is renowned for its diverse culinary delights, and while exploring the local cuisine is a must, it is crucial to be cautious about food and water safety. Stick to eating at reputable establishments and avoid street vendors whose hygiene practices may be questionable. Ensure that fruits and vegetables are thoroughly washed, and opt for bottled water or boiled water to stay hydrated.

3. Mosquito-Borne Diseases:

Malaysia, being a tropical country, is home to mosquitoes that may transmit diseases such as dengue fever, Zika virus, and chikungunya. To protect yourself, wear long sleeves, use insect repellents, and stay in accommodations with proper mosquito screens. Additionally, empty any standing water around your living space to eliminate mosquito breeding grounds.

4. Heat and Sun Safety:

The Malaysian climate can be hot and humid, particularly during certain months. To avoid heat-related illnesses, such as heatstroke or dehydration, drink plenty of fluids, wear loose and breathable clothing, and use sunscreen with a high SPF. Seek shade and avoid excessive sun exposure, especially during the peak hours of the day.

5. Traffic and Road Safety:

When exploring Malaysia, it is essential to be cautious on the roads. Traffic can be chaotic, and road conditions may vary. Always use designated pedestrian crossings, be vigilant when crossing roads, and consider using reputable transportation services. If you plan to rent a vehicle, familiarize yourself with local traffic rules and drive defensively.

6. Emergency Services and Travel Insurance:

Before your trip, ensure that you have adequate travel insurance that covers medical expenses and emergency evacuations. Familiarize yourself with the contact information for emergency services in Malaysia, including the local police, medical facilities, and your embassy or consulate.

Conclusion:

By being aware of the common health risks and safety tips in Malaysia, you can minimize potential hazards and enjoy a memorable trip. Remember to take necessary precautions, stay informed, and prioritize your well-being throughout your journey. With proper planning and awareness, your visit to Malaysia will be a delightful experience while ensuring your health and safety.

Chapter 37: Travel Insurance for Malaysia

Introduction:

Traveling to Malaysia is an exciting adventure that offers breathtaking landscapes, vibrant cultures, and delicious cuisine. However, it is crucial to prioritize your safety and well-being while exploring this beautiful country. One way to ensure a worry-free journey is by obtaining travel insurance. In this chapter, we will discuss the benefits of travel insurance for Malaysia and guide you on how to purchase the right coverage for your trip.

Understanding the Benefits of Travel Insurance:

1. Medical Coverage:

Accidents and illnesses can happen unexpectedly, even during a vacation. With travel insurance, you can have peace of mind knowing that you are protected against medical emergencies. This coverage includes hospitalization, medical treatments, and emergency medical evacuation, ensuring that you receive the best possible care without worrying about exorbitant expenses.

2. Trip Cancellation or Interruption:

Life is unpredictable, and unforeseen circumstances may force you to cancel or cut short your trip. Travel insurance provides coverage for trip cancellation or interruption due to various reasons such as illness, injury, natural disasters, or even unexpected work commitments. You can recover the non-refundable expenses and additional costs incurred due to these unfortunate situations.

3. Lost or Delayed Baggage:

Imagine arriving in Malaysia only to find out that your luggage has been lost or delayed. Travel insurance offers coverage for such incidents, reimbursing you for essential items and clothing until your baggage is recovered. This ensures that you can continue your journey comfortably without being burdened by the inconvenience caused by lost or delayed baggage.

4. Personal Liability:

Accidents happen, and sometimes they can involve other people. Travel insurance provides personal liability coverage, protecting you against legal expenses and compensation claims if you accidentally cause injury to someone or damage their property. This coverage ensures that you are financially protected in case of unforeseen accidents or incidents.

5. Emergency Assistance:

Being in a foreign country can be overwhelming, especially during emergencies. Travel insurance offers 24/7 emergency assistance services, providing you with immediate help and guidance in case of any unforeseen situations. Whether you need medical advice, assistance with lost documents, or emergency travel arrangements, the insurance company will be there to support you throughout your journey.

How to Purchase Travel Insurance for Malaysia:

1. Research and Compare:

Start by researching reputable insurance providers that offer travel insurance coverage for Malaysia. Compare their plans, benefits, and prices to find the one that best suits your needs and budget. Look for companies with good customer reviews and a reliable claims process.

2. Determine Your Coverage Needs:

Consider the activities you plan to engage in during your trip to Malaysia. If you are planning adventurous activities such as scuba diving or hiking, ensure that your travel insurance covers these specific activities. Assess your medical needs, trip duration, and the value of your belongings to determine the appropriate coverage for your trip.

3. Read the Policy Details:

Before purchasing travel insurance, carefully read the policy details, terms, and conditions. Pay close attention to coverage limits, exclusions, and any pre-existing medical conditions that may affect your coverage. Ensure that the policy aligns with your travel plans and provides comprehensive coverage for your specific requirements.

4. Purchase in Advance:

It is recommended to purchase travel insurance as soon as you book your trip to Malaysia. This ensures that you are covered for any unforeseen events that may occur before your departure. Waiting until the last minute may limit your coverage options or result in higher premiums.

5. Keep Documentation Handy:

Once you have purchased travel insurance, keep a copy of the policy documents, contact numbers, and emergency assistance details easily accessible during your trip. This will help you quickly access the necessary information in case of an emergency or when filing a claim.

Conclusion:

Travel insurance is an essential aspect of any trip to Malaysia. By understanding the benefits it offers and following the steps to purchase the right coverage, you can explore this captivating country with confidence, knowing that you are protected against unexpected events. Prioritize your safety, well-being, and peace of mind by securing travel insurance for your Malaysian adventure.

Chapter 38: Learning the Language of Malaysia

Introduction:

Malaysia is a diverse and multicultural country, home to various ethnic groups such as Malays, Chinese, and Indians. With such diversity, the country boasts a rich linguistic heritage, with Bahasa Malaysia being the national language. Learning the language of Malaysia can enhance your travel experience, allowing you to communicate with locals, understand the culture more deeply, and navigate through the country with ease. In this chapter, we will explore the resources available for learning Bahasa Malaysia, ensuring an enjoyable and immersive language learning journey.

1. Language Schools:

One of the most effective ways to learn Bahasa Malaysia is by enrolling in a language school. Malaysia offers a wide range of language institutes that cater to both beginners and advanced learners. These schools provide structured courses taught by experienced teachers who specialize in teaching the language to foreigners. With interactive lessons, cultural immersion activities, and personalized attention, language schools offer a comprehensive learning experience.

2. Online Language Learning Platforms:

In today's digital age, online language learning platforms have gained immense popularity. These platforms provide flexibility and convenience, allowing learners to study at their own pace and from anywhere in the world. Numerous websites and mobile applications offer Bahasa Malaysia courses, incorporating interactive exercises, audiovisual materials, and virtual language exchange opportunities. Additionally, many platforms provide forums and chat groups where learners can practice their language skills with native speakers.

3. Language Exchange Programs:

Language exchange programs provide a unique opportunity to learn Bahasa Malaysia while simultaneously teaching your native language to a local Malaysian. These programs foster cultural exchange and allow learners to practice their language skills in real-life situations. Various organizations and communities organize language exchange events, where participants can engage in conversations, share their knowledge, and build friendships with locals. Such programs offer an authentic and immersive language learning experience.

4. Language Learning Apps:

Mobile applications have revolutionized language learning, making it accessible to anyone with a smartphone or tablet. There are several language learning apps available that offer Bahasa Malaysia courses tailored to different proficiency levels. These apps utilize gamification techniques, allowing learners to earn points, unlock levels, and compete with friends, making the learning process engaging and enjoyable. Additionally, many apps provide pronunciation guides, flashcards, and quizzes to enhance language retention.

5. Cultural Immersion:

Immersing yourself in the local culture is an invaluable way to learn Bahasa Malaysia. Engaging in cultural activities, such as visiting local markets, attending traditional festivals, or staying with a Malaysian host family, provides an immersive language learning experience. By surrounding yourself with native speakers, you can practice your language skills in real-life situations and gain a deeper understanding of the language's nuances, idioms, and expressions.

Conclusion:

Learning the language of Malaysia, Bahasa Malaysia, opens doors to a deeper understanding of the country's culture, history, and people. Whether you choose to enroll in a language school, utilize online platforms, participate in language exchange programs, or immerse yourself in the local culture, the resources available for learning Bahasa Malaysia are plentiful. By embracing these resources and dedicating time and effort, you will embark on a rewarding language learning journey that will enhance your travel experience and create lasting memories in Malaysia.

Chapter 39: Tips for Traveling with Children in Malaysia

Traveling with children can be an exciting and fulfilling experience, especially when exploring the vibrant and diverse country of Malaysia. With its stunning landscapes, rich cultural heritage, and family-friendly attractions, Malaysia offers endless opportunities for memorable adventures. To ensure a smooth and enjoyable trip, here are some essential tips for traveling with children in Malaysia.

1. Pack Smartly:

When traveling with children, it's crucial to pack wisely. Start by bringing comfortable clothing suitable for the tropical climate, including lightweight and breathable fabrics. Don't forget to pack sunscreen, insect repellent, and hats to protect your little ones from the sun. Additionally, include essential medications, first aid supplies, and any special items your child may need, such as diapers, formula, or favorite toys.

2. Choose Child-Friendly Accommodations:

When selecting accommodations in Malaysia, opt for child-friendly hotels or resorts that offer amenities catering to families. Look for establishments with spacious rooms, swimming pools, playgrounds, and even kid's clubs. These facilities will provide your children with plenty of entertainment and opportunities to make new friends during your stay.

3. Embrace Malaysian Cuisine:

One of the highlights of visiting Malaysia is indulging in its diverse and delicious cuisine. However, children can sometimes be picky eaters. To ensure your child enjoys the local fare, look for restaurants that offer a variety of options, including familiar dishes like chicken rice, noodles, or fresh fruit. Additionally, remember to pack some of your child's favorite snacks for times when they may not be keen on trying new foods.

4. Explore Family-Friendly Attractions:

Malaysia boasts numerous attractions that are perfect for children of all ages. Kuala Lumpur, the capital city, offers exciting experiences such as the Petronas Twin Towers, the KL Bird Park, and the Aquaria KLCC. If you're looking for a more natural setting, head to Borneo, where you can visit the Sepilok Orangutan Rehabilitation Centre or explore the Kinabatangan Wildlife Sanctuary. These destinations provide unique opportunities for children to learn about wildlife conservation and experience the wonders of nature up close.

5. Be Mindful of Safety:

While Malaysia is generally a safe country to visit, it's essential to prioritize your child's safety during your travels. Keep an eye on your children at all times, especially in crowded areas or near bodies of water. Ensure they are wearing appropriate safety gear when participating in water activities or adventure sports. Familiarize yourself with emergency contact numbers and the location of nearby medical facilities, just in case.

6. Engage with the Local Culture:

Malaysia is a melting pot of diverse cultures, and engaging with the local culture can be a fantastic learning experience for children. Encourage your little ones to interact with locals, try traditional games, or learn a few basic phrases in the local language. Visiting cultural sites such as temples, museums, and markets will also provide valuable insights into Malaysia's heritage.

Remember, traveling with children requires flexibility and patience. Take breaks when needed, maintain a relaxed pace, and allow your children to participate in planning activities. By following these tips, your family's journey through Malaysia will undoubtedly be filled with unforgettable moments and cherished memories.

Chapter 40: Tips for Traveling with Seniors in Malaysia

Introduction:

Traveling with seniors can be a rewarding and memorable experience. Malaysia, with its diverse culture, stunning landscapes, and warm hospitality, is an excellent destination for senior travelers. However, it's important to plan ahead and consider the specific needs and preferences of seniors to ensure a smooth and enjoyable trip. In this chapter, we will provide you with valuable tips on what to pack, where to stay, and things to do when traveling with seniors in Malaysia.

1. Packing Essentials:

When traveling with seniors, it's crucial to pack wisely to ensure their comfort and safety. Here are some essential items to consider:

a) Medications: Make sure to bring an ample supply of any prescribed medications, along with a copy of the prescription.

b) Comfortable Clothing: Pack lightweight and breathable clothing suitable for the tropical climate. Include comfortable walking shoes and a hat for protection against the sun.

c) First Aid Kit: Carry a basic first aid kit with essentials like band-aids, antiseptic cream, pain relievers, and any necessary medical supplies.

d) Travel Insurance: It's advisable to have comprehensive travel insurance that covers any unforeseen medical emergencies or travel disruptions.

2. Choosing Accommodation:

Selecting the right accommodation is vital when traveling with seniors. Consider the following factors:

a) Accessibility: Opt for hotels or resorts that offer accessible features such as ramps, elevators, and rooms with grab bars or handrails.

b) Location: Choose accommodations that are centrally located, close to tourist attractions, medical facilities, and public transportation.

c) Facilities: Look for hotels that provide amenities like wheelchair accessibility, senior-friendly bathrooms, and on-site restaurants.

d) Safety: Prioritize accommodations with good security measures, well-lit areas, and 24-hour front desk services.

3. Sightseeing and Activities:

Malaysia offers a plethora of exciting activities and attractions suitable for seniors. Here are a few suggestions:

a) Cultural Experiences: Visit the vibrant city of Kuala Lumpur and explore iconic landmarks like the Petronas Twin Towers, National Mosque, and Batu Caves. Immerse yourself in the rich cultural heritage of Georgetown in Penang, known for its historical sites and mouthwatering cuisine.

b) Nature Escapes: Take a leisurely boat ride through the mangroves of Langkawi or enjoy a peaceful walk in the lush Cameron Highlands. The Taman Negara National Park offers guided tours and wildlife spotting opportunities.

c) Relaxation: Treat your seniors to a rejuvenating spa experience in one of Malaysia's renowned wellness retreats. Head to the pristine beaches of Langkawi or the idyllic islands of Perhentian for a tranquil getaway.

d) Food Exploration: Malaysia is a paradise for food lovers. Sample the diverse flavors of Malaysian cuisine, from street food stalls to upscale restaurants. Consider taking a food tour to discover the country's culinary delights.

Conclusion:

Traveling with seniors in Malaysia can be an enriching experience filled with unforgettable moments. By packing wisely, choosing suitable accommodations, and planning activities that cater to their needs, you can ensure a comfortable and enjoyable trip. Remember to prioritize their safety and well-being, and embrace the unique cultural and natural wonders that Malaysia has to offer.

Chapter 41: Tips for Traveling Solo in Malaysia

Traveling solo can be an incredibly rewarding experience, allowing you to immerse yourself in the vibrant culture and natural beauty of Malaysia at your own pace. However, it's important to take certain precautions to ensure your safety and make the most out of your trip. In this chapter, we will provide you with valuable tips on where to stay, things to do, and how to stay safe while traveling solo in Malaysia.

1. Choosing Accommodation:

When traveling alone in Malaysia, it's crucial to select accommodation that offers a safe and comfortable environment. Opt for reputable hotels, guesthouses, or hostels that have positive reviews and are located in well-populated areas. Check if they have security measures in place, such as CCTV cameras, 24-hour reception, and secure locks on doors.

2. Exploring the Cities:

While traveling solo in Malaysia, you'll have the opportunity to explore vibrant cities like Kuala Lumpur, Penang, and Melaka. Make sure to visit popular tourist attractions during daylight hours when there are more people around. Be cautious of your belongings and avoid displaying expensive items that may attract unwanted attention. It's also wise to familiarize yourself with local customs and dress modestly to respect the cultural norms.

3. Discovering Nature:

Malaysia is renowned for its stunning natural landscapes, from lush rainforests to pristine beaches. When venturing into nature alone, always inform someone about your plans and expected return time. Stick to marked trails and be aware of any potential risks, such as wildlife encounters or changing weather conditions. Carry sufficient water, insect repellent, and sunscreen to ensure a comfortable and safe experience.

4. Public Transportation:

Public transportation in Malaysia is generally safe and efficient. Utilize trains, buses, or ride-hailing services like Grab to get around the cities. Avoid traveling alone late at night, especially in secluded areas. If you're taking a taxi, use only licensed ones and ensure the driver uses the meter. It's wise to have the address of your destination written down or saved on your phone to avoid any language barriers.

5. Engaging with Locals:

One of the joys of solo travel is the opportunity to interact with locals and learn about their culture. Malaysians are known for their warm hospitality, so don't hesitate to strike up conversations or seek recommendations. However, exercise caution and maintain personal boundaries, especially with strangers. Trust your instincts and be aware of common scams to avoid any unpleasant situations.

6. Staying Connected:

Having a reliable means of communication is essential when traveling alone. Purchase a local SIM card upon arrival or activate an international roaming plan with your service provider. This will allow you to stay connected with loved ones and access important information, such as maps and emergency contacts. Additionally, inform someone back home about your itinerary and regularly check in with them to ensure your well-being.

7. Personal Safety:

While Malaysia is generally a safe destination, it's important to remain vigilant and take necessary precautions. Avoid walking alone in dimly lit or isolated areas, especially at night. Keep your belongings secure and be cautious of pickpockets in crowded places. It's advisable to carry a photocopy of your passport and important documents while leaving the originals in a safe place. In case of an emergency, dial 999 for immediate assistance.

By following these tips, you can make your solo adventure in Malaysia a memorable and safe experience. Embrace the diversity, natural wonders, and warm hospitality that this beautiful country has to offer. Happy travels!

Chapter 42: Tips for Traveling on a Budget in Malaysia

Introduction:

Traveling on a budget doesn't mean compromising on the quality of your experience. Malaysia, with its diverse culture, stunning landscapes, and delicious cuisine, offers numerous opportunities for budget travelers to explore and enjoy. In this chapter, we will provide you with valuable tips on where to stay, things to do, and how to save money while traveling in Malaysia.

1. Affordable Accommodation Options:

a) Hostels: Malaysia has a wide range of hostels that offer comfortable and affordable accommodation. Hostels are not only budget-friendly but also provide an opportunity to meet fellow travelers and exchange travel tips.

b) Guesthouses: Guesthouses are another great option for budget travelers. They offer basic amenities, a friendly atmosphere, and are usually located in convenient areas.

c) Homestays: Experience the local culture and save money by opting for homestays. Many Malaysians open their homes to travelers, providing a unique opportunity to immerse yourself in Malaysian hospitality.

2. Exploring on a Budget:

a) Free Attractions: Malaysia boasts several free attractions that allow you to experience the beauty of the country without spending a dime. Visit the iconic Petronas Twin Towers in Kuala Lumpur or explore the vibrant street art in Penang.

b) Nature Trails: Malaysia is blessed with breathtaking natural landscapes. Take advantage of the numerous nature trails and hiking routes available across the country. From the Cameron Highlands to

Taman Negara, there are plenty of opportunities to explore the great outdoors for free or at a minimal cost.

c) Cultural Experiences: Immerse yourself in Malaysia's rich cultural heritage by visiting temples, mosques, and cultural villages. These experiences are often affordable or have a nominal entrance fee.

3. Budget-Friendly Eateries:

a) Hawker Centers: Malaysia is renowned for its vibrant street food culture. Head to hawker centers, where you can savor a variety of local dishes at affordable prices. From mouth-watering satay to flavorful nasi lemak, you'll find an array of delicious options.

b) Local Markets: Explore the local markets and food stalls to sample authentic Malaysian cuisine at a fraction of the cost of a restaurant meal. Don't miss the bustling night markets, which offer a wide range of street food and affordable souvenirs.

4. Transportation Savings:

a) Public Transportation: Malaysia has an efficient and affordable public transportation system. Utilize buses, trains, and trishaws to get around major cities. This not only saves money but also provides an opportunity to experience the local way of life.

b) Ride-Sharing Services: Ride-sharing services like Grab are widely available in Malaysia. They offer a convenient and cost-effective way to travel within cities or between destinations.

c) Shared Transportation: Consider sharing transportation costs with fellow travelers. Joining group tours or sharing taxis can help reduce expenses while exploring popular tourist spots.

Conclusion:

Traveling on a budget in Malaysia is not only feasible but also rewarding. By choosing affordable accommodation, exploring free attractions, indulging in local cuisine, and utilizing cost-effective transportation options, you can make the most of your Malaysian adventure without breaking the bank. Remember, traveling on a budget doesn't mean compromising on the quality of your experience;

it means discovering unique ways to enjoy Malaysia's beauty while saving money along the way.

Chapter 43: Tips for Traveling Responsibly in Malaysia

Introduction:

As a responsible traveler, it is essential to be aware of the impact we have on the environment and culture of the places we visit. In this chapter, we will explore some valuable tips to help you minimize your impact while traveling in Malaysia. By following these guidelines, you can ensure a more sustainable and respectful experience, allowing you to create lasting memories while preserving the beauty and integrity of this remarkable country.

1. Respect the Local Culture:

Malaysia is a diverse country with a rich cultural heritage. To travel responsibly, it is crucial to respect and appreciate the local customs, traditions, and beliefs. Take the time to learn about the different cultures and religions present in Malaysia, and be mindful of your behavior and attire when visiting religious sites or conservative areas. Engage with locals, ask questions, and always seek permission before taking photographs of people or their properties.

2. Support Local Businesses:

When planning your trip to Malaysia, make a conscious effort to support local businesses, including accommodations, restaurants, and souvenir shops. By doing so, you contribute directly to the local economy and help preserve the authenticity of the destination. Opt for locally owned hotels or guesthouses, dine at family-run restaurants, and purchase souvenirs made by local artisans. This way, you can have a more meaningful experience while empowering the local communities.

3. Reduce Plastic Waste:

To minimize your environmental impact, it is important to be mindful of your plastic consumption. Malaysia, like many other countries, faces challenges with plastic pollution. Carry a reusable water bottle and refill it at water stations or by boiling tap water. Say no to plastic straws and bring your own reusable shopping bag. Additionally, be conscious of your waste disposal and use recycling facilities whenever available.

4. Choose Sustainable Transportation:

Malaysia offers various transportation options, and selecting sustainable alternatives can significantly reduce your carbon footprint. Consider taking public transportation, such as buses or trains, which are not only eco-friendly but also allow you to immerse yourself in the local culture. If renting a vehicle, choose a fuel-efficient or electric car. In cities, opt for walking or cycling tours to explore the surroundings, promoting a healthier lifestyle while reducing air pollution.

5. Conserve Natural Resources:

Malaysia is blessed with breathtaking natural beauty, from lush rainforests to stunning coastlines. As a responsible traveler, it is crucial to conserve these precious resources. Respect wildlife and their habitats by observing from a safe distance and refraining from feeding or touching them. Conserve water by taking shorter showers and reusing towels. When hiking or exploring nature trails, stay on designated paths to avoid damaging fragile ecosystems.

Conclusion:

By following these tips for traveling responsibly in Malaysia, you can help preserve the environment and culture of this incredible country. Remember, responsible travel is not only about personal enjoyment but also about leaving a positive impact on the places we visit. By respecting local customs, supporting local businesses, reducing plastic waste, choosing sustainable transportation, and conserving natural resources, you can ensure a more sustainable and meaningful travel experience in Malaysia.

www.ingramcontent.com/pod-product-compliance
Lightning Source LLC
Chambersburg PA
CBHW051220160726
47994CB00002B/676